PERSONAL LIBRARY
OF ROYCE DICKINSON, JR

ENNIS AND NANCY HAM LIBRARY
ROCHESTER COLLEGE
800 WEST AVON ROAD
ROCHESTER HILLS, MI 48307

What Shall We Do With The Bible?

by
Rubel Shelly, M.A.

NATIONAL CHRISTIAN PRESS, INC.
P. O. Box 1001   Jonesboro, Ark. 72401

Copyright by
Thomas B. Warren
1975

Contents

		Page
	INTRODUCTION	v
	PREFACE	ix
I.	MODERN MAN PONDERS AN ANCIENT BOOK	1
II.	THE BIBLE PRESENTS ITS OWN CASE	10
III.	PREDICTIVE PROPHECY AS PROOF OF THE BIBLE'S SUPERNATURAL ORIGIN	18
IV.	THE UNITY OF THE BIBLE AS PROOF OF ITS SUPERNATURAL ORIGIN	30
V.	THE SCIENTIFIC ACCURACY OF THE BIBLE AS PROOF OF ITS INSPIRATION	38
VI.	THE UNIQUENESS OF THE BIBLICAL VIEW OF THINGS AS AN EVIDENCE OF INSPIRATION	46
VII.	THE TESTIMONY OF ARCHAEOLOGY TO THE TRUSTWORTHINESS OF THE BIBLE	57
VIII.	ARE THERE ERRORS IN SCRIPTURE?	67
IX.	ALLEGED ERRORS IN THE OLD TESTAMENT	78
X.	ALLEGED ERRORS IN THE NEW TESTAMENT	93
XI.	THE TRANSMISSION AND TRANSLATION OF SCRIPTURE	114
XII.	THE VALUE OF SACRED SCRIPTURE	125
	FOOTNOTES	132

To My Parents

Mr. and Mrs. James P. Shelly
with eternal love
and gratitude

Introduction

In this brief introduction, I want to refer to two things: (1) the subject matter and (2) the author of this book. There is a very real sense in which I take pride in both.

We are living during a time of great skepticism. Many men now living have lost their concept of the world as having been created for a purpose. To many people today, the world is "just there," and that is all there is to it. Because many men have ceased to view the world as teleological (designed and created for a *purpose*), they have lost their concept of God as *creator*. Because they have lost their view of God as creator, they have lost their conviction that *truth* is *absolute*. Because of their loss of conviction as to absolutes, many have come to view *the Bible* as nothing but a *human* document. As a result of such a concept, many men have come to view morality and religion as nothing but products of mere human invention. That such is not the case (but rather, the Bible is the product of the infinite God) is shown by the author of this book.

It has long been a three-fold abiding passion of mine: (1) to develop the basic argument which would prove without doubt that the Bible is the inspired, infallible, and authoritative word of God, (2) to help younger men to see this truth, and (3) to encourage them to communicate this truth to others by means of oral speech, journal articles, tracts, and books.

I am convinced that I did develop the basic argument for such proof. I have set forth that argument (with full proof that the premises of that argument are true) in the classroom. I also have set forth in print the basic argument (first, in a journal article[1] and, second, in a lecture[2] during a college lectureship). I am more than a little pleased that one of my students, Rubel Shelly, is now giving an extended treatment of this basic argument and some of the supportive evidence. In addition he has dealt with a number of items to which we were not able to give much attention in the classroom.

To be a teacher in any sense of the real meaning of that word is to be concerned for the development and work of the students involved. There can hardly be a greater joy to a teacher than to see a student do well. It is an even greater joy to see a student excel. As a student in quite a number of my courses, Rubel Shelly has been a student of unusual ability, and, even though he is still young in years, he already has written a number of very valuable books in addition to a number of well-written tracts and journal articles. For a time he served ably as associate editor of the journal whch I edit (*The Spiritual Sword*). In that capacity, he made great contributions both as an associate editor in the formulations of the basic structure of the journal and in the writing of various articles. In the writing of this present book, he makes a great contribution to these and other past accomplishments.

To write a good book is to extend the good which one can accomplish hundreds—perhaps thousands—of times over. In writing this book the influence of Mr. Shelly will be extended many times. In an age of growing skepticism and of the increase of moral and spiritual chaos, nothing can be quite so effective in turning civilization to the right direction as (1) the proclamation and proof of the existence of God, and (2) the proclamation and proof of the fact that the Bible is the word of God. I am convinced that the author, in the writing of this book, has accomplished the second of these all-important matters. In the light of this

---

[1] Thomas B. Warren. "The Bible is Inspired and Authoritative—Our Basic Argument." *The Spiritual Sword*, Vol. 1, No. 2.

[2] Thomas B. Warren. "The Bible is God's Word—The Meaning of and Basis for This Claim." Flatt, West, Warren, eds. *The Inspiration and Authority of the Bible*. (Gospel Advocate Co., Nashville, 1971.)

conviction, I commend this book to the reading public with the expectation, the Lord willing, that other valuable works will be coming from the same pen.

>THOMAS B. WARREN, PH. D.
>Professor, Philosophy of Religion &
>Christian Apologetics
>Harding Graduate School of Religion
>Memphis, Tennessee 38117
>October 1, 1974

Preface

This book is one more of many already produced by apologists for the Christian faith. If others have been written before and by men far abler than this author, what justification is there for the presentation of this particular volume to the public?

It is felt that this book is unique in that it offers not only a number of facts relevant to the subject of the inspiration and authority of the Bible but also *presents the logical tool* which demonstrates that these facts *demand the conclusion that the Bible is from God*. Many writers set forth facts without bothering to incorporate them in a logical argument. In the strictest sense of the term, such a parading of data without logical structure does not "prove" anything at all. A thousand pages of facts may not justify the conclusion claimed by their compiler; only when the facts are presented within the framework of a valid argument is any conclusion justified and established. I am indebted to Dr. Thomas B. Warren for helping me appreciate the necessity of logical formulation; he has been my most helpful teacher and friend who has read the manuscript for this book but who, of course, is not to be held responsible for any of its weaknesses.

This book can be viewed as a totality and be regarded as an argument for the inspiration and authority of the Scripture. The total argument may be stated as follows:

1. If it is the case that the Bible contains predictive prophecies which were clearly made in advance of their unquestioned fulfillment, is character-

ized by a humanly impossible unity, treats matters of science in a way which transcends human invention in the days when its various parts were written, has a view of reality otherwise unknown in human thought, has been confirmed by all the accepted means of historical research (e.g., archaeology), and is free from demonstrable error (as well as possessing other features which are beyond mere human wisdom or invention) then the Bible is the Word of God.
2. The Bible contains predictive prophecies which were clearly made in advance of their unquestioned fulfillment, is characterized by a humanly impossible unity, treats matters of science in a way which transcends human invention in the days when its various parts were written, has a view of reality otherwise unknown in human thought, has been confirmed by all the accepted means of historical research (e.g., archaeology), and is free from demonstrable error (as well as possessing other features which are beyond mere human wisdom or invention).
3. Therefore the Bible is the Word of God.

Yet each chapter in the book can be seen to stand on its own as proof of the Bible's divine origin. For example, the chapter on predictive prophecy sets forth an argument which is adequate of itself to establish the inspiration of the Bible. Each chapter can be studied profitably for its own argument; the cumulative force of all the chapters together constitutes a far weightier argument than any single element within it.

It is my earnest hope and prayer that this book will be a useful tool in helping the skeptic come to faith and in undergirding the faith of one who has long placed his confidence in Scripture without having examined in detail the solid evidence upon which that faith rests.

The Bible is the Word of God! This I hold not by a "leap of faith" (i.e., beyond what the "hard evidence" demands as a conclusion) but on the basis of evidence which *demands* that Scripture be so regarded. This is not merely a "more reasonable view" of the Bible than any other; it is the only possible view in light of the evidence at hand.

CHAPTER I

Modern Man Ponders An Ancient Book

The Bible is a product of antiquity and therein lies a great problem! How can a book as old as this possibly be relevant to the present situation of man? Can a man writing 700 years before the birth of Christ really tell us anything which is crucial to life in the space age? Can Paul, living in a world of first-century scientific backwardness, interest us as much as today's newspaper? Can literature which deals with events of the distant past offer "news" to modern man? Such questions as these are crucial to twentieth-century people who, like the people of ancient Athens, "spend their time in nothing except telling or hearing something new." (Acts 17:21 RSV).

Furthermore, the Bible has come to us through fallible human beings. It was not handed down directly from heaven. Its central figure, Jesus Christ, did not write a single book within it. Without exception, every part of the Bible came from the pens of men who were imperfect. How, then, can anyone contend that the finished product of these human beings is itself infallible and inerrant? This line of thought has convinced many moderns that although the Bible may be "God's Word" in some limited sense it is necessarily marred by the defects which are common to human imperfection.

The Bible is relevant to modern man if—and ONLY if —it is inspired by God. Only if the very words of this book originated with deity can we be confident that it has a meaningful message to us.

Isaiah, Paul and the other human writers of the Bible could not have seen into the future so as to make their writings meaningful to men who would live centuries after their times; but the all-knowing God who created man in his own image could see the end from the beginning and could therefore speak with authority to men of antiquity and modern times in one and the same sentence!

Errant and fallible men could have written an inerrant and infallible Bible if—and only if—God exerted some extraordinary divine influence upon them. Drawing upon the highest wisdom of their times, Bible writers could not have avoided making glaring errors in their pronouncements; but the all-powerful God who unfailingly accomplishes his purposes could so control men as to reveal truth *through* them which would not be marred *by* them!

The Bible claims to be a document produced by just such supernatural means. For example, Peter said that the message of the Old Testament prophets did not come "by the will of man: but men spake from God, being moved by the Holy Spirit." (2 Pet. 1:21).

Mankind's Dilemma Over the Bible

A professor of theology at Harvard Divinity School has voiced modern man's dilemma over the Bible in a very candid manner. After granting the profound impact it has had on Western civilization and on man's spiritual life in particular, he writes:

> But all this is over with and gone. Though we may recognize and be grateful for its contributions to our culture, the Bible no longer has unique authority for Western man. It has become a great but archaic monument in our midst. It is a reminder of where we once were—but no longer are. It contains glorious literature, important historical documents,

exalted ethical teachings, *but it is no longer the word of God (if there is a God)* to man.[1]

This quotation adequately expresses the impossible position in which so many contemporary theologians find themselves. They realize that they are necessarily involved with the Bible by virtue of their heritage and profession, but they feel that it is now very much like a millstone about their necks! Since they do not believe the Bible is what it claims to be—and since they are not even sure there is a personal God whose favor man is to seek—they do not find any practical place for it in their religious lives or teachings. Thus Christianity has become, for them, simply another philosophical system and something other than the one true religion.

Although the average man might not express his feelings about the Bible in so sophisticated a manner as a Harvard theologian, it is nevertheless true that he is caught up in the same dilemma. He has come to regard the Bible as a book for the linguistic and historical experts. It is an antiquated volume with no practical value for our modern and complex world. He no longer believes that God is speaking to him through the Bible.

The prevailing attitude toward the Bible is not belief but unbelief. Skepticism has become the order of the day and the objective truth of the gospel is hidden in the mists of human subjectivism and relativism. Christ has become a dim figure of the past and no one is sure who he was, what he did or what he meant to do.

The Bible has been attacked, maligned and discredited by countless critics. At the same time all this has been going on, its professed friends have held their peace and have failed to counter the assaults upon the Word of God. The field of intellectual and spiritual combat has largely been abandoned to the destructive critics and their speculative philosophical systems.

Is it true that the Bible has been shown to be merely a human production? Has it been demonstrated that Scripture is filled with errors and self-contradictions? Is it true that all educated people have seen insufficiencies in the Bible? No, we simply are living at a time when the prevailing thought systems are such as to contradict the system set forth in the Bible. And men are more willing to be tossed to and fro with the winds of the time than to believe, declare and defend the truth which has been given us by God!

The Bible is not a purely human production. It is a God-breathed revelation of truth through specially chosen and enabled men. The Bible is not filled with errors and self-contradictions. There is not even one error—whether pertaining to history, science or theology—anywhere in the Word of God. And it is not true that all educated people disbelieve the Bible, for many intelligent minds which have honestly investigated the evidence are confirmed believers in its validity and power.

The Christian Response to This Dilemma

The time has come for Christians to come out of hiding and to challenge the world with the truth which God has entrusted to us. "But sanctify in your hearts Christ as Lord: being ready always to give answer to every man that asketh you a reason concerning the hope that is in you, yet with meekness and fear." (1 Pet. 3:15.) Believers are under obligation to press a strong case for Christ and the gospel and to defend that case against all attacks. We have been disobedient to God in this respect. We have shrunk back into a naive world of pietistic subjectivism and have tried to pretend that we can maintain faith in spite of the critics' denials and counter claims.

This hesitation and shrinking back on the part of Christians has led many to conclude that the arguments set forth by the enemies of Christ are unanswerable. Many have thus abandoned their faith and countless others are haunted by constant doubts. Many who once regarded the Bible as the Word of God to man now hesitate to acknowledge any acquaintance with it lest they be ridiculed as uninformed and unintelligent people who persist in holding on to something which has been falsified by modern critical research.

This generation is one which questions and probes. Men are not content to accept what their fathers believed

—about the universe, medicine, religion or anything else —just because their fathers believed it. Some Christians lament this spirit and feel that it will be the undoing of the gospel system. God rejoices over it! He has always challenged men to put him to the test, for the historical and intellectual foundations beneath the gospel are sound. Long ago he challenged the followers of false gods: "Produce your cause, saith Jehovah; bring forth your strong reasons, saith the King of Jacob." (Isa. 41:21). One who challenges others to present convincing proof of their claims implies an eager willingness to do so for his own! Such is still the sentiment of our God!

The gospel of Jesus Christ is rational and intelligent. A man does not have to take his intelligence out of gear in order to find it appealing. He does not have to abandon his tough-minded desire to know the truth when he examines its claims and supporting evidences.

The New Testament does not ask men to commit themselves to something unproved and unprovable. It asks only that they consider the evidence for its case and make a rational decision concerning it. It presents credible evidence which, when examined according to the accepted rules of evidence and logic, can be recognized as totally trustworthy.

It just will not do to say that the intellectual objections to the Bible cannot be answered but as a "blind leap of faith" we will accept it anyway. Such a notion is foreign to our innate sense of reason. It is also foreign to the spirit of the Bible itself. The writers of the Bible held that truth is to be intellectually considered in the broad daylight of honest investigation or else it is nothing. Paul contended that the resurrection of Christ was physical, capable of historical proof and statable in human language. Otherwise, he conceded, the Christian faith must be declared untrue and vain. (Cf. 1 Cor. 15). The same attitude must be held with regard to the Bible. If it is not capable of defense on historical, scientific and logical grounds, the Christian faith must be declared untrue and vain!

There simply is no Christian religion without an objectively verifiable Bible, for Christianity arises from its statements of historical fact, moves toward the goal envisioned in its clear promises and gives meaning to life in the here and now. "But we have renounced the hidden things of shame, not walking in craftiness, nor handling the word of God deceitfully; but by the manifestation of the truth commending ourselves to every man's conscience in the sight of God. And even if our gospel is veiled, it is veiled in them that perish: in whom the god of this world hath blinded the minds of the unbelieving, that the light of the gospel of the glory of Christ, who is the image of God, should not dawn upon them." (2 Cor. 4:2-4).

Nature and Plan of This Book

This book belongs to that class of literature termed *apologetic*. Christian apologetics is that realm of study which submits proofs in support of the truthfulness of the Christian religion. It is a systematic argument in defense of the divine origin and authority of Christianity. It contends that it is possible for men to know that Christianity is the one religion approved of God. Its objective is to set forth such evidence as will constitute proof of the truthfulness of Christianity and to consider and answer the challenges which are offered to it. And what modern man needs is not less apologetics but more!

The gospel of Jesus Christ appeals to the total man— both heart and intellect. And until the gospel is presented in light of this fact we need not be surprised to find its message falling on many deaf ears.

This book attempts to make a contribution to apologetics with special regard to the Bible. Its thesis is that the Bible alone is the written Word of God to man, infallible and inerrant as originally given.

Positively, it will be shown that the Bible is a book which can be explained only on the basis of supernatural influence. This will involve a consideration of such things as predictive prophecy, the Bible's treatment of scientific matters, its complete historical trustworthiness, etc. Negatively, it will be shown that the Bible does not contain errors and self-contradictions which would serve to bring it down to the level of a human production.

Factors Weighing Against This Effort

At the very beginning of such a study, it must be realized that this sort of effort is opposed by the spirit of the age in which we live. Our world has drawn a sharp line between belief and knowledge, between faith and fact. Philosophically this dates back to Kant and Kierkegaard and expresses itself in existential philosophy and neo-orthodox theology.

Although the writings of neo-orthodox theologians are often very vague, on their attitude toward the infallibility of Scripture they are quite clear. Emil Brunner has written: "The orthodox doctrine of Verbal Inspiration has been finally destroyed."[2] He has also charged that the Bible is full of errors, contradictions, erroneous opinions concerning all kinds of human, natural and historical situations. C. H. Dodd has frankly declared: "We no longer accept a saying as authoritative because it lies before us as a word of Jesus."[3] And perhaps none has been so bold in his pronouncements as Karl Barth. He flatly charges that

> . . . the prophets and apostles as such, even in their office, even in their function as witnesses, were real, historical men as we are, and therefore sinful in their action, and capable and actually guilty of error in their spoken and written word.[4]

Neo-orthodox theology makes man the measure of Scripture and its authority. The Word of God thus becomes a subjective experience for man and not an objective revelation! If a given passage strikes a responsive chord in the heart of a neo-orthodox theologian, he will declare it inspired and accept it. If it does not appeal to him, he will reject it out of hand! Lest this appear to be too sweeping a statement, hear Dodd again: "Sometimes I think Paul is wrong, and I have ventured to say so. In the main, what he says seems to me to be profoundly true."[5] This concept of authority in religion does not even require that we have a Bible, for an individual with such an attitude as these men is obviously determined to chart his own course in religion without being bound by the Bible.

On a more popular level, this spirit speaks of "the leap of faith" and thereby implies that the Christian religion is to be accepted only because it offers an alternative to the pessimism and despair of world reality and not because it is capable of being proved true. This theme appears again and again in the sermons and writings of modern religious leaders. Such an attitude rejects the notion that history and reason are sufficient grounds for one's decision to follow Christ. It says, in effect, that historical criticism and logical investigation are not even capable of application to matters of faith.

This attempted separation of fact from faith is entirely false. It is fatal to Christianity, for its appeal to man's heart is made through the avenue of his mind! And those who want to hold Christian faith independently of sound evidence will ultimately come to a state of abject despair in religion, for the heart cannot rejoice in what the mind rejects. Reason itself is a divine gift and is capable of distinguishing between truth and error in affirmations of the Christian faith. (Cf. 1 John 4:1; 1 Thess. 5:21).

Neither will it be adequate for someone to cry, "My faith is in Jesus Christ and not in the book which tells me about him!" All that we know of God's revelation of himself through Christ comes from the Scripture; therefore it is foolish to propose some sort of separation of the two. Jesus made no such distinction himself. He rested his claims for himself upon the Word of God and constantly appealed to its authority.

Satan is undoubtedly pleased to see men depreciating the role of reason in religion. He has seen many a serious and honest inquirer approach some Christian and call him to account for his faith. He has trembled in the fear that the Christian is prepared to make a defense. Then he has laughed with glee to see the Christian dismiss his questioner with a form of false piety and protest that his faith does not rest on the faulty foundation of logic and reasoned argument!

A Final Observation

As we offer the Bible to men of our age, we must keep in mind that something is needed in addition to a reasoned presentation concerning its origin and nature. There needs to be a demonstration of the Bible's relevance to human life in the day-to-day conduct of believers! It will not do to pay lip service to the truthfulness of Scripture and assume that logic and common sense are all we need.

Merely subscribing to a particular set of beliefs about the Bible—that it is inspired, inerrant, the very Word of God to man—falls short of what God desires from us. For, while all these propositions are true, belief in the Bible as God's Word is not so formal a matter. We must always approach the Bible in terms of its *authoritative content* and be "doers of the word." (Cf. James 1:22-25). The Pharisees of Jesus' day believed in and defended the inspiration of the Old Testament, but this did not keep them from terrible apostasy from God! Lest the same fate befall us, let us speak to critics of the Bible with both logical argument and personal subjection to the message of the book.

Conclusion

What is *your* estimation of the Bible?

If you hold the Bible in high esteem as the infallible Word of God, you will take care to learn, believe and live by the truths contained in it. If you view the Bible as a human production which, though valuable as literature, is filled with myths and errors, you will certainly have an altogether different attitude. Your opinion of the Bible and its worth is therefore all-important.

In the course of reading and studying the material in this book you will be given an opportunity to evaluate a case for the infallibility of the Bible and think deeply about its authority for your life.

CHAPTER II

The Bible Presents its Own Case

Every courtroom has had liars testify on its witness stand. Yet judges still allow men to come into their courts and tell their own stories! Why? Surely the answer is obvious enough: not all men are liars. Honest men tell the truth, and it is upon the basis of truth told by honest men that justice is done. So, in a courtroom, every man is allowed to testify so as to set forth his own case. But it is understood that his testimony will not be accepted without adequate supporting evidence.

In this chapter we shall assume that the Bible is on the witness stand and that the reader of this book is hearing its testimony about itself. It is understood that you will not grant the Bible's claims just because those claims have been made. You will require adequate supporting evidence for them—and that evidence will be forthcoming in the subsequent chapters of this book.

Someone may object immediately by saying that this procedure begs the question. It may be alleged that this is circular reasoning which says, "I believe the Bible is inspired and inerrant because it claims to be; and I believe its claims because they are found in an inspired and inerrant book." This, of course, would not be a valid form of argument. But such is not the argument of this chapter.

This chapter seeks only to establish the Bible's claims about itself and leaves to further investigation the determination of the truth or falsity of such claims.

To ignore the Bible's claims would be a terrible mistake. For example, what if the Bible actually admits that it is not an infallible book? There would be nothing more to say in behalf of the thesis of this book! Or what if the Bible simply makes no claim to being inspired? The unbeliever could then say that to claim inspiration for the Bible is to press a claim which is not inherent in the book itself and is thus going beyond the evidence at hand. If, on the other hand, the Bible does make an explicit claim to inspiration, fairness will demand that we examine the claim in the light of all the available evidence.

Dewey M. Beegle has asserted: "We need to remind ourselves that the verbal plenary formulation of inspiration is, after all, only a doctrine—a non-Biblical doctrine at that."[1] If this assertion is true, the thesis set forth in the first chapter of this book can never be established. William Sanday, though not applying the principle consistently in his own work, has correctly observed that "we may lay it down as a fundamental principle that a true conception of what the Bible is must be obtained from the Bible itself."[2]

What does the Bible claim for itself?

The Claims of the Old Testament

The speakers and writers involved in producing the Old Testament clearly laid claim to divine control over their pronouncements. They never hesitated to claim infallibility for their message and to give it the very authority of God!

The central figure of the Old Testament is Moses. When God first appeared to him and made known his intention of using him as the deliverer of Israel, Moses made excuses for himself. He claimed a lack of experience in public affairs and lamented that he would not know what to say. "And Moses said unto Jehovah, Oh, Lord, I am not eloquent, neither heretofore, nor since thou hast spoken unto thy servant; for I am slow of speech, and of a slow tongue. And Jehovah said unto him, Who hath made man's mouth? or who maketh a man dumb, or deaf, or seeing, or blind? is it not I, Jehovah? Now therefore go, and *I will be with thy mouth,* and teach thee what thou shalt speak." (Ex. 4:10-12).

Not only does the Old Testament claim that Moses *spoke* by divine authority and under divine control but also that he *wrote* under the same influence. "And Jehovah said unto Moses, Write this for a memorial in a book . . ." (Ex. 17:14). "And Moses wrote all the words of Jehovah . . ." (Ex. 24:4). "And Jehovah said unto Moses, Write thou these words: for after the tenor of these words I have made a covenant with thee and with Israel." (Ex. 34:27).

The first five books of the Old Testament are attributed to Moses. And no less than 420 times in these books is it declared that the express words of God are being conveyed!

The same type of claim is constantly made for the prophets of the Old Testament. The words "Thus saith the Lord" or their equivalent appear approximately 80 times in the book of Isaiah alone. Jeremiah wrote: "Then Jehovah put forth his hand, and touched my mouth; and Jehovah said unto me, Behold, I have put my words in thy mouth." (Jer. 1:9). The uniform testimony of the prophets was that they spoke only when the Lord gave them his word. (Cf. Hos. 1:1; Amos 1:3; Mic. 1:1; Mal. 1:1; *et al.*).

One cannot help noticing that these claims specify that God is the author of the very words which the men spoke and wrote. He did not merely inspire their thoughts and leave them to express infallible divine concepts in fallible human rhetoric. In fact, such a notion is unthinkable when one realizes that thoughts and concepts are transmitted only by means of words! If God enlightened the minds of these men at all, he did so by means of words.

Jesus' Claims for the Old Testament

Even more important than the claims of Old Testament personalities about themselves and their statements is the testimony of Jesus Christ about them. How unthinkable it is for a person to profess faith in Christ and, at the same time, admit that he does not view the Scriptures as he viewed them!

Of the Old Testament writings Jesus said, "The scripture cannot be broken." (John 10:35). The word translated "broken" in this verse is a common one which is used of breaking a law. It means to annul, deny or withstand its authority. Jesus thus stated a fact which he regarded as a self-evident truth concerning Scripture. It is impossible to withstand the Scripture, for it is infallibly true in every detail and possesses absolute authority.

In the Sermon on the Mount, he said, "Think not that I came to destroy the law or the prophets: I came not to destroy, but to fulfil. For verily I say unto you, Till heaven and earth pass away, one jot or one tittle shall in no wise pass away from the law, till all things be accomplished." (Matt. 5:17-18).

The "jot" (or *yodh*) to which Jesus referred in this statement is the smallest letter of the Hebrew alphabet and resembles an apostrophe in English. The "tittle" is a small projection on a Hebrew letter which changes it from one letter to another. It is somewhat similar in nature to the little line which changes an O into a Q. Therefore Jesus was contending that the smallest letter and even the smallest part of a letter in "the law or the prophets" (a common designation of Jesus' time which stood for the entire Old Testament) must be fulfilled.

> Nothing could be plainer than this, that in the smallest details he regards the law as incapable of being made void and that in the smallest details it is taken up by him and finds, in his fulfillment of it, its permanent embodiment and validity. By the most stringent necessity there is but one conclusion, namely, that the law is infallible and inerrant.[3]

CLAIMS FOR THE NEW TESTAMENT

Not only did Jesus indicate his complete confidence in the Old Testament but he also placed his stamp of approval on the New Testament—even in advance of its production! He promised the apostles: "Howbeit when he, the Spirit of truth, is come, he shall guide you into all the truth: for he shall not speak from himself; but what things soever he shall hear, these shall he speak: and he shall declare unto you the things that are to come." (John 16:13). Notice two important things about this statement from Jesus. First, he called the Holy Spirit "the Spirit of truth." Surely this signifies that the Spirit's revelation to the apostles would be altogether without error and therefore the truth. Second, he promised that the Spirit would guide them "into all the truth." He was not to communicate some truth along with some error. Jesus said he would guide them into the truth, the whole truth and nothing but the truth!

That the apostles and other writers of the New Testament considered themselves to have received the fulfillment of this promise is evident from their own statements. They never had the least shadow of doubt as to the exact truthfulness of their words! Paul gratefully acknowledged that the Thessalonians had accepted his teaching "not as the word of men, but, as it is in truth, the word of God . . ." (1 Thess. 2:13). Paul boldly affirmed to the Corinthians that "what I am writing to you is a command from the Lord." (1 Cor. 14:37 RSV). Peter contended that the apostles "preached the gospel unto you by the Holy Spirit sent forth from heaven." (1 Pet. 1:12).

Paul, Peter and the other New Testament writers did not view themselves as mere fallible witnesses to a series of the acts of God in history. They were witnesses, yes; but they were more! They were witnesses who had been enabled to declare the meaning of God's actions and the subsequent responsibilities of men to God!

Two Classic Texts

No examination of the Bible's claims for itself would be complete without a careful consideration of 2 Timothy 3:16-17. "All scripture is inspired by God and profitable for teaching, for reproof, for correction, and for training in righteousness, that the man of God may be complete, equipped for every good work." (RSV). Paul did not say that Scripture is inspiring—although that would have been true. He was not describing the effect of Scripture on man. He was rather talking about the effect of God's work on Scripture. All Scripture is "God-breathed"—for this is the literal meaning of the word translated "inspired by God."

Paul had no doubt as to the ultimate authorship of Scripture. God produced it! Therefore it is to be accepted as being fully authoritative. As to its purpose, he declared that Scripture was able to make one "complete, equipped for every good work." This means that nothing is lacking in it which is necessary for man! And to assert that "all scripture" (or "every single passage of scripture") is "profitable for teaching, for reproof, for correction, and for training in righteousness" is certainly to claim inerrancy, for if Scripture were part truth and part error such a claim would be meaningless. Indeed, if that were the case, Scripture would *need* correction rather than *give* correction.

Next consider Peter's statement to the effect that "no prophecy ever came by the will of man: but men spake from God, being moved by the Holy Spirit." (2 Pet. 1:21). Peter claimed that the writers of Scripture were not free to select whatever words they wished as they gave—orally or in writing—their prophecies. Instead they were "moved" or "borne along" by the Holy Spirit. The Greek word here is the same one used in Acts 27:17 of Paul's ship on the voyage to Rome which was "driven" or "borne along" by the strong winds of a storm. The inspired writers no more determined their course in writing than the ship determined its course amidst such strong winds!

This teaches that the writers of Scripture did not have ultimate control over what they wrote, but the Holy Spirit determined the end product. This is not to say that the human writers were mere robots or mechanical devices. But it is to say that the ultimate choice of the very words they wrote down was not their own but the Holy Spirit's.

Summing up the Bible's claims about itself, we should note that human authorship of the individual parts is freely and fully granted. Yet the human authors are not regarded as the source of their statements. The origin, truthfulness and authority of Scripture are due to God's power exercised through these specially chosen men.

Furthermore, the human authors are nowhere regarded as impairing the message which God gave them, for God's overruling influence was so great as to keep them from all error. Thus the Bible claims to have the authority of God's own voice being heard from on high! It is God's very word to man and "cannot be broken."

A Negative Consideration

Before leaving this matter of the Bible's case for itself, let us give attention to one type of negative evidence which speaks for the infallibility and inerrancy of Scripture. Although the fact is frequently overlooked, it is important to the thesis of this chapter to observe that Scripture nowhere calls itself into question. No part of the Bible criticizes another part. No passage declares some other to be in error. And this is all the more remarkable when one realizes that approximately 40 different men were involved in writing its separate parts over a period of about 1600 years!

Would anyone be surprised to find a scientist writing today and exposing some theory which was proposed in 1970? Are physicians of today still advocating the same theories of medical practice which were in vogue in the 1800s? Philosophical thought proceeds on the basis of antithesis. Today's philosopher takes the many statements of past men in his area of study and challenges, questions and discards until he feels that he has arrived at a more acceptable conclusion. And where could we find forty theologians who would feel no compulsion to criticize each other?

Yet Paul cannot be found calling Isaiah into question. Daniel nowhere contradicts Moses in any matter. Peter is under no compulsion to bring the antiquated theories of some ancient Biblical writer up to date.

Conclusion

Any number of theories about the Bible and its nature have been advanced by men. Modernists hold that the Bible *contains* the Word of God, but that it also contains the errors of its human writers. This view makes each individual the final judge of spiritual truth and necessitates an arbitrary judgment between the divine truth and the human error that Scripture is alleged to include. The neo-orthodox theory is that the Bible *becomes* the Word of God at whatever time its message takes on meaning to an individual. This view denies the objective truthfulness of the Bible and is totally subjective. Some Fundamentalists view the Bible as having been *dictated* word for word by God into the ears of men who were nothing more than transcribing secretaries. This does not account for the stylistic peculiarities of the various men who did the writing of Scripture. Still others contend for a type of *thought inspiration* which allowed the various writers to express God's will in the best manner of which they were capable. This weakens the Bible's authority, for we could never know how accurate these men were in their efforts.

The Bible's own case is that God gave certain men both the thoughts and the words which accurately expressed his will. At the same time, while exercising this type of thorough control over the writers, he allowed for their own personalities, vocabularies and writing styles to be in evidence. Thus the Bible claims to be the authoritative Word of God which has been given as a revelation to mankind. It claims to be not a mere recording of the events of history but the unfolding of God's purpose in those events. The Bible claims to be God's Word, not man's. It admits to have come *through* man but denies being *of* man.

Does the evidence support or deny these claims? The Bible has been heard to testify in its own behalf and now we shall turn to an examination of the evidence which relates to its claims.

CHAPTER III

Predictive Prophecy as Proof of the Bible's Supernatural Origin

As was pointed out in the previous chapter, the mere stating of a claim does not guarantee its truthfulness. The Bible claims to be the infallible and inerrant Word of God to man in propositional form. It claims to be the authoritative standard for life in this world and holds forth promises and threats relative to an existence which is to follow earthly life. Is there adequate supporting evidence to justify these bold claims? The thesis of this book obviously presupposes that sufficient evidence does exist to prove the Bible to be everything it claims to be. Some, but by no means all, of the proofs of inspiration will now be set forth.

Traditionally an appeal has been made to *external* and *internal* evidences of the inspiration of the Bible. External evidences consist of demonstrations of the factuality of the Biblical record in the light of geography, culture, history, archaeology, etc. But it should be pointed out that conformity to fact does not prove inspiration.

Whereas an inspired book would necessarily be historically and geographically accurate, other books might meet these tests and still be uninspired. For example, a carefully documented history of the United States might fully conform to the facts but the man who wrote it would not have been guided by the Holy Spirit. External evidences are thus seen to be confirmatory in their nature rather than of primary significance.

These comments about external evidences have not been made in an effort to minimize their importance, but to underscore the fact that *the case for Biblical inspiration and authority must be made from the book itself.* Internal evidences must be forthcoming which will unmistakably demonstrate the supernatural character of the book. This evidence must be so compelling as to demand the conclusion that human intelligence could not have produced the Bible and that, in fact, only God could have done so!

It is therefore contended that the Bible not only *claims* to be the inspired and authoritative Word of God but also *justifies that claim in its very nature.*[1]

BASIC STATEMENT OF THE ARGUMENT

Biblical prophecy concerning future events is a unique and arresting phenomenon of history. And, like any other historical fact, it demands an explanation. Although the enemies of Christianity have used every conceivable device and argument in an attempt to discredit these prophecies and to set them aside, they have failed in the effort. The predictive prophecies of the Bible are matters of clear historical record and the events that fulfilled those predictions are equally clear matters of record! If the prophecies were not inspired of God, what explanation is there for them?

The Bible itself places great emphasis on predictive prophecy as proof of the truthfulness of the total system of things revealed therein. The following challenge was issued to the idol-gods of Babylon in the time of Isaiah: "Let them bring them forth, and declare unto us what shall happen: declare ye the former things, what they are, that we may consider them, and know the latter end of them; or show us things to come. *Declare the things that are to come hereafter, that we may know that ye are gods . . .*" (Isa. 41:22-23a).

While challenging the dumb idols of the heathen to do that which clearly was not within their power, the ability of Jehovah to accurately predict the future is held forth as a clear vindication of his power. "Remember the former things of old: for I am God, and there is none else; I am God, and there is none like me; *declaring the end from the beginning, and from ancient times things that are not yet done;* saying, My counsel shall stand, and I will do all my pleasure." (Isa. 46:9-10).

The basic argument which will serve as the foundation for all else which follows in this chapter can be formally stated in the following form:[2]

(1) All predictive prophecies which can be explained solely on the basis of supernatural influence and which were clearly made known before their corresponding fulfillments are evidences (proofs) which verify the claims of the religion involved.
(2) All predictive prophecies recorded in the Bible are predictive prophecies which can be explained solely on the basis of supernatural influence and which were made known before their corresponding fulfillments.
(3) Therefore, all predictive prophecies recorded in the Bible are evidences (proofs) which verify the claims of the religion involved.

Since one of the claims of the Christian religion is the possession of a God-breathed and authoritative Bible, the establishment of the argument presented above will constitute logical certainty of the Bible's inspiration.

As Bernard Ramm has pointed out, this argument from prophecy "is essentially the argument from omniscience. Limited human beings know the future only if it is told them by an omniscient Being."[3]

Definition and Characteristics of Predictive Prophecy

The fundamental meaning of the word prophecy is not prediction, but the *speaking forth of the mind of God*. It is the declaration of that which could not have been known by natural means. It is "the forth-telling of the will of God, whether with reference to the past, the present, or the future . . ."[4]

But the forth-telling of the will of God frequently involved the foretelling of events which were to come to pass in the distant future. In this study we are concerned only with the predictive element of Bible prophecy.

M'Ilvaine has given a very useful definition of predictive prophecy as ". . . a declaration of future events, such as no human wisdom or forecast is sufficient to make—depending on a knowledge of the innumerable contingencies of human affairs, which belongs exclusively to the omniscience of God; so that from its very nature prophecy must be divine revelation."[5]

It should be pointed out that before a statement can legitimately be classified as prophetic in character it must be more than just a good guess based on high probability. For example, from careful examination of issues, potential candidates and public opinion, one might be able to predict who the next President of the United States will be. There would, however, be nothing astonishing or truly "prophetic" about such a prediction. But if a man living in Egypt 2500 years ago had prophesied about the United States, named the man who will be our next president, given the name of his opponent, the margin of his victory and the policies he would enact, *that* would have been true predictive prophecy.

Neither are scientific predictions of eclipses or atmospheric phenomena to be considered prophetic. Such forecasts are merely statements of confidence in nature's continued and orderly functioning. They have a basis in observable and verifiable data as such information relates to natural laws. On the other hand, true prophecy is frequently of such a nature as to be in exact opposition to what human experience and reason would predict.

This leads us to a consideration of the characteristics of Biblical prophecy as contrasted with pseudo-prophecy. True prophecy must be evaluated in the light of three definite criteria.

First, the prophecy must deal with nations, persons and/or events that are, at the time of the prophetic utterance, remote enough in time so as to be incapable of mere guesswork or logical deduction. This criterion requires that a prophecy be the foretelling of an event far enough removed in time that the prophet cannot have an immediate part in its actual occurrence and that it be of such a nature as to exclude all elements of chance.

Second, true prophecy is not a matter of vague generalizations which can later be applied to a situation in a questionable manner, but frequently involves minutely detailed predictions. People are named and their destinies are carefully traced long before they are even born. Nations are characertized before they exist and wars are described before they are fought. The more detailed the prophecy and the more unusual its nature, the greater its evidential value.

Third, the fulfillment of the prophecy must be clear and unequivocal. Mere prediction is no evidence of supernatural presence and power. It is the clear fulfillment of the prediction in an unmistakable fashion that proves its divine character.

EXAMPLES OF BIBLICAL PROPHECIES

An amazing group of prophecies found in the Bible relate to the overthrow of specific cities and nations of antiquity and to the future of the Jews.

Babylon

In the day of Babylon's glory, Isaiah prophesied of its total desolation. That ancient city was surrounded by a wall wide enough for three chariots to be driven abreast on its top. Its hanging gardens was one of the seven wonders of the ancient world. It had paved streets, running water and many of the conveniences which we associate with modern cities. Yet Isaiah spoke for God (in the eighth century B.C.) and said: "Behold, I will stir up the Medes against them, who shall not regard silver, and as for gold, they shall not delight in it. And their bows shall dash the young men in pieces; and they shall have no pity on the fruit of the womb; their eye shall not spare children. And Babylon, the glory of kingdoms, the beauty of the Chaldeans' pride, shall be as when God overthrew Sodom and Gomorrah. It shall never be inhabited, neither shall it be dwelt in from generation to generation: neither shall the Arabian pitch tent there; neither shall shepherds make their flocks to lie down there. But wild beasts of the desert shall lie there; and their houses shall be full of doleful creatures; and ostriches shall dwell there, and wild goats shall dance there. And wolves shall cry in their castles, and jackals in the pleasant palaces: and her time is near to come, and her days shall not be prolonged." (Isa. 13:17-22).

The prophet must have been thought to be a madman by those who heard and read his prediction. How could the world's richest and greatest city become totally desolate? But for two thousand years now, history has stood as irrefutable confirmation of the inspiration of Isaiah's prophecy!

The Medes came against Babylon in 539 B.C. and, under the leadership of Cyrus, conquered it. Its destruction was made complete when Cyrus' son-in-law, Xerxes, later plundered the city. So desolate did Babylon become that, when Alexander the Great later decided to restore it, he gave up the task as a hopeless one!

Tyre

Against ancient Tyre, Ezekiel gave this prophecy: "Therefore thus saith the Lord Jehovah, Behold, I am against thee, O Tyre, and will cause many nations to come up against thee, as the sea causeth its waves to come up. And they shall destroy the walls of Tyre, and break down her towers: I will also scrape her dust from her, and make her a bare rock. She shall be a place for the spreading of nets in the midst of the sea; for I have spoken it, saith the Lord Jehovah; and she shall become a spoil to the nations . . . And I will make thee a bare rock; thou shalt be a place for the spreading of nets; thou shalt be built no more: for I Jehovah have spoken it, saith the Lord Jehovah." (Ezek. 26:3-5, 14).

Nebuchadnezzar led a siege against Tyre which lasted for thirteen years. The mainland city was destroyed as a result of that siege and the people of Tyre fled to an island which was about one-half mile off shore. The Tyrians felt safe, for Nebuchadnezzar had no ships and could not follow them. There the city existed until 332 B.C. Alexander the Great came against Tyre and, in a most ingenious manner, overcame the problem which had stalled Nebuchadnezzar. He tore down the ruins of the old mainland city and used its stones, timbers and topsoil to construct a land bridge over to the island! Even this, however, was in fulfillment of prophecy. Ezekiel had said of Tyre's enemies: "They shall lay thy stones and thy timber and thy dust in the midst of the waters." (Ezek. 26:12). And today the site of the old mainland city is nothing more than barren rock where fishermen can be seen to spread their nets! The city has never been rebuilt!

Nineveh

Nineveh is another example of a city whose future was foretold accurately through the prophets of God. Approximately one hundred to one hundred fifty years after Nineveh's penitence under the preaching of Jonah, her sinfulness again became so great that God had the prophets Nahum and Zephaniah to speak of her impending doom. "And he will stretch out his hand against the north, and destroy Assyria, and will make Nineveh a desolation, and dry like the wilderness. And herds shall lie down in the midst of her, all the beasts of the nations: both the pelican and the porcupine shall lodge in the capitals thereof; their voice shall sing in the windows; desolation shall be in the thresholds: for he hath laid bare the cedar-work. This is the joyous city that dwelt carelessly, and said in her heart, I am, and there is none besides me: how is she become a desolation, a place for beasts to lie down in! every one that passeth by her shall hiss, and wag his hand." (Zeph. 2:13-15; cf. Nah. 1:1-8).

In 612 B.C. the combined forces of the Babylonians and Medes came against Nineveh and completely destroyed it. The once proud and powerful city was in ruins and was an object of derision and scorn!

The Jews

Of special interest to the student of the Bible are the prophecies related to the future of the Jewish people.

Frederick the Great of Prussia is said to have asked his court chaplain to give him the evidence for the Bible's inspiration in a word. The chaplain is reported to have answered, "The Jews." Indeed, the Jews do furnish strong evidence of the supernatural origin of the Bible.

Ezekiel, speaking for God, said, "And I will scatter thee among the nations, and disperse thee through the countries . . ." (Ezek. 22:15). The observant person realizes that his prophecy has been fulfilled. Jeremiah said they would be scattered among nations "whom neither they nor their fathers have known." (Jer. 9:16). Witness the large Jewish population in America as proof of this accurate prediction. Jeremiah further said that the Jews would become "a reproach and a proverb, a taunt and a curse, in all places where I shall drive them." (Jer. 24:9). The sad fulfillment of this true prediction is known to everyone.

Were these prophecies merely the recorded ravings of men who were angry with their own people? Did it just coincidentally happen that their predictions came true? If the prophecies were few and far between, that explanation might be acceptable. If *some* of their predictions came to pass and others failed, such a theory might be justified. But the complete fulfillment of every one of this great number of prophecies points to a supernatural origin!

Prophecies About Christ

No more concrete evidence of the Bible's reliability as a prophetic book could be cited than the many detailed prophecies concerning Jesus Christ which have been accurately fulfilled. Ordinarily one's biography is written after he has lived. The life story of Jesus was written generations before his birth!

The place of his birth was foretold in Micah 5:2. The prophecy was made that his mother would be a chaste, unmarried woman—i.e., a virgin. (Isa. 7:14). The work of John the Baptist, his forerunner, was announced in Malachi 3:1. His triumphal entry into Jerusalem was foretold in Zechariah 9:9. His death and its purpose were outlined by Isaiah. (Isa. 53). The dividing of his personal belongings and the casting of lots for his seamless garment were predicted in Psalm 22:18.

The New Testament records an episode of conversion which is rooted in the Old Testament prophecy contained in Isaiah 53. The evangelist Philip proclaimed Jesus to be the fulfillment of this detailed prophecy of Jehovah's Suffering Servant. Although a popular alternative to Philip's inspired interpretation of Isaiah 53 identifies the Servant as Israel, this is not a reasonable possibility for the following reasons: (1) Isaiah 49:5-6 clearly distinguishes between the Servant and Israel, (2) Israel suffered because of her own sins (cf. Deut. 28) whereas the Servant of Isaiah 53 suffered as an innocent victim, (3) Israel was not a voluntary sufferer as was the Servant and (4) Israel's sufferings did not atone for the sins of mankind.

One should also notice that Isaiah 53 is capable of satisfying every test which can be legitimately applied to determine a prophecy's supernatural origin. It undeniably antedates the time of Christ by several hundred years and deals with events which could not have been either guesses by the author or contrived fulfillments by its subject. It is magnificently specific and cannot be dismissed on grounds of vagueness or ambiguity. And the fulfillment of Isaiah 53 is unequivocal in every particular.

The first nine verses of Isaiah 53 contain nine clear prophecies concerning Jesus Christ. First, verse one predicts that the Servant would be rejected and that his message would not be believed. Fulfillment of this is seen in such events as those related in John 12:37-43. Second, verse two anticipates some of the reasons which would underlie his rejection by the people. The fact that Jesus was a rather rustic person from an unpromising corner of the land who lacked any royal "comeliness" or carnal "beauty" did contribute to prejudice against him and his ultimate rejection by many. (Cf. John 1:46-47).

Third, verse three states that he would be "despised and rejected of men; a man of sorrows, and acquainted with grief." The fulfillment of this part of the prophecy is so well known as to require no comment. (Cf. Luke 18:31-32). Fourth, verses four, five and nine indicate that he was to bear the sins of others, although he was personally guiltless before God. That the New Testament writers claimed that Jesus' death was indeed a vicarious death of the Righteous One for the sinful multitude is unmistakable. (Cf. 2 Cor. 5:21). Fifth, verse six indicates that he was to be the instrument for calling the Father's straying sheep back into the fold. Jesus used this representation of his mission in John 10 and clearly viewed himself as pointing men back to his Father.

Sixth, verse seven states that the Servant would suffer in silence. He would be harassed and mistreated by his enemies, but he would be submissive to their evil assaults and would not resist their efforts. This is exactly what took place on the night of his betrayal and during the subsequent hours of his trials and execution. (Matt. 26:60-63; 27:12-14; Mark 14:60-61). So impressive was this aspect of his conduct that Peter commented on it in 1 Peter 2:21-25—over 35 years after the events themselves. Seventh, verse eight predicts that oppressive and unjust proceedings would deny justice to the Servant. The four or five "trials" of Jesus were mockeries of the law and common human decency.

Eighth, verse nine prophesies that he would make his grave with the wicked. This was fulfilled in the fact that he was crucified in the company of two criminals. But, ninth, the same verse also holds forth the seemingly contradictory prospect of his being "with a rich man in his death." This was fulfilled in his burial in the tomb of the rich Joseph of Arimathea. (Matt. 27:57-60).

In all, there are over 330 prophecies in the Old Testament which relate to the birth, life, ministry, death and resurrection of Christ. How can we account for these detailed prophecies which were written hundreds of years before Christ was born? How can we explain the fact that every one was fulfilled to the letter? They were the inspired utterances of Spirit-filled men! "Someone has taken the trouble to calculate that the possibility of their being fulfilled in one person by sheer chance is one over 84,000,000,000,000,000,000,000,000,000,000,000,000,000,000,000,000,000,000,000,000,000,000,000,000,000,000,000,000,000,000,000,000,000,000,000,000,000,000,000,000th of 1 per cent."[6]

Arguments Against Prophecy

But if the prophecies of the Bible are so clearly supernatural in their nature why are there any who refuse the claims of Christianity? Are there not objections made to the argument from predictive prophecy? Certainly so. There are three such arguments against the significance of predictive prophecy which are of specially weighty influence.

First, it is sometimes contended that the alleged prophetic statements are so vague as to be capable of application to whatever situation may arise in history. For example, if someone were to predict that an evil man will try to destroy the United States in the next twelve months, he could then identify almost any person he chose as the fulfillment of his prophecy—anyone from the president to a radical political activist. It is claimed that the prophecies of the Bible are of this vague type.

While it must certainly be granted that some prophecies are less specific as to the identification of persons, places and events than others, it cannot be shown that all Bible prophecies are obscure. To the contrary, there are many examples of names, times and circumstances having been stated with startling exactness which simply cannot be dismissed on this ground. The examples given in this chapter are of such a specific character.

Second, it has been claimed that the prophecies of the Old Testament have been artificially fulfilled. Again, it is possible that one could go to a place or assume a name which has been specified in a prophetic utterance and claim to be the fulfillment of it. For example, a man could go to Bethlehem for the birth of his child and claim fulfillment of Micah 5:2. But the fact remains that most of the Bible's prophecies are of such a nature as to be beyond the possibility of an artificially arranged fulfillment. How could the prophecies about the rise and fall of nations have been controlled so as to bring about their artificial fulfillment?

Third, one of the favorite evasions of the force of predictive prophecy by the so-called "higher critics" is to date the writing of the alleged prediction after the event which it purports to foretell. It is certainly to be granted that the dating of Biblical materials is not absolutely certain in every case, but the dating of books in periods after the major prophetic events have already taken place is an action of arrogant prejudice. The liberal critic rules out the possibility of the supernatural and is then forced to assign a date to the book in question which will put it in a later period. Yet it can be shown that even when the late dates are consistently granted for all the Old Testament materials there still remains a large enough body of prophecies to establish a conclusive case for the claims of Christianity. For example, all the prophecies about Christ clearly antedated his birth by several hundred years at the least.

Conclusion

Let the honest inquirer examine the prophecies of the Bible. He will inevitably be led to the conclusion that only the wisdom and power of God could account for them.

CHAPTER IV

The Unity of the Bible as Proof of its Supernatural Origin

An important consideration with regard to the internal evidences of the inspiration of the Bible is its remarkable *unity*. Over a period of time comparable in length with the time from the Roman emperor Constantine to the present (i.e., approximately 1600 years), a group of about forty different men from all parts of the civilized world and from altogether contrasting backgrounds wrote sixty-six books in three different languages which exhibit a humanly impossible unity of teaching and structure. Considered collectively, these sixty-six books constitute *one book* with *one message*. No explanation short of divine inspiration has ever been offered which explains this phenomenon adequately!

As one author has observed:

> A thousand men may work on a great cathedral, and even take centuries to build it, but if it comes out a work of art, the foundation fittingly suited to the

minarets, spires and windows, it is certain there was an architect back of the planning and the building.

... If a fragment of stone were found in Italy, another in Asia Minor, another in Greece, another in Egypt, and on and on until sixty-six fragments had been found, and if when put together they fitted perfectly together, making a perfect statue of Venus de Milo, there is not an artist or scientist but would arrive immediately at the conclusion that there was originally a sculptor who conceived and carved the statue. The very lines and perfections would probably determine which of the great ancient artists carved the statue. Not only the unity of the Scriptures, but their lines of perfection, suggest One far above any human as the real author. That could be no one but God.[1]

This quotation serves to express the argument of this chapter in a very simple and clear way. And as we line up various pieces of evidence to support the thesis of this book, the fact of the unity of the Bible must not be overlooked.

Stated in a more logically precise form, the argument to be developed in this chapter would take the following form:

(1) If it is the case that the Bible demonstrates a unity of teaching and structure which could not be achieved by unaided human effort, then its origin must be traced to a single supernatural source (i.e., God).

(2) It is the case that the Bible demonstrates a unity of teaching and structure which could not be achieved by unaided human effort.

(3) Therefore the Bible's origin must be traced to a single supernatural source (i.e., God).

UNITY OF THEME

As one first looks at the Bible he is impressed by its diversity. Here are many different books written by many different men from many different historical settings. But as he looks more deeply into the Bible, he discerns an unmistakable unity of theme and purpose which is nothing short of amazing!

The *theme* of the Bible is *the redemption of sinful man by means of God's grace*. The story begins in Genesis with the account of man's creation and subsequent fall. Redemption was *required* by man's sinful rebellion against his Creator. This is related in the opening chapters of Genesis. Redemption was then *prepared for* by means of God's promise to Abraham and the constitution of Israel as his chosen people through whom the Messiah and Savior would come. This narrative begins with the twelfth chapter of the book of Genesis and is traced in detail through the historical books of the Old Testament. Redemption was next *prophesied* through the various Old Testament writers who foretold the coming of the Messiah, his suffering for the sins of others and the establishment of his glorious kingdom.

Redemption *became reality* by means of the events related in the first four books of the New Testament. Jesus Christ was born of a virgin, lived a sinless life among men for over thirty years, died on the cross for the sins of others, rose from the dead on the third day and ascended back to heaven to sit on the throne of David in regal splendor. Redemption was then *proclaimed and shared* by the apostles and prophets of the early church. The book of Acts tells how the gospel was preached to the Jews first and then to the Gentiles. It pictures the rapid spread of the kingdom of God among men. Redemption is *explained* and its implications are sketched in the epistles (i.e., Romans through Jude) of the New Testament. Finally, redemption is *ultimately realized* in the book of Revelation, the book which assures God's children of their final and complete victory over the world and its evils.

UNITY OF STRUCTURE

Because of the unity of theme and purpose in all the parts of the Bible, there is an obvious unity of structure about the book as a whole. "The New Testament is in the Old concealed; the Old Testament is in the New revealed." This old and familiar statement is profoundly true.

One can see an obvious link between the Old and New Testaments in spite of the four-hundred-year period between them. For example, Malachi closes the Old Testament with a prediction of the next major event in the divine schedule—the appearance of the Messiah and his forerunner. "Behold, I send my messenger, and he shall prepare the way before me: and the Lord, whom ye seek, will suddenly come to his temple; and the messenger of the covenant, whom ye desire, behold, he cometh, saith Jehovah of hosts." (Mal. 3:1). Again, the same prophet wrote of the Messiah's forerunner that he would come in the spirit of Elijah: "Behold, I will send you Elijah the prophet before the great and terrible day of Jehovah come. And he shall turn the heart of the fathers to the children, and the heart of the children to their fathers; lest I come and smite the earth with a curse." (Mal. 4:5-6).

Moving to the New Testament, one sees that the coming of John the baptizer was regarded as the "beginning of the gospel of Jesus Christ, the Son of God." (Mark 1:1). John came in the spirit and power of Elijah and sought to prepare a people for the Messiah who was to come. (Cf. Luke 1:17). He preached, "Repent ye, for the kingdom of heaven is at hand." (Matt. 3:3).

When you go to see a movie, you will be shown "coming attractions" by the management of the theater. The purpose of this is to advertise future offerings and to get you into a frame of mind to return to that theater when these movies arrive. This sort of advertisement is both commonplace and effective. This is precisely what God did in overseeing the production of the Bible. The Old Testament closes with a preview of "coming attractions" so that we would understand the process of revelation was not yet completed. More would come later. It did come in the form of the New Testament and the entirety of this revelation is now in our hands! We have it as a single unit of divine revelation with every part fitting into its proper place in the structure of the whole!

The tie between the Old and New Testaments is further emphasized in the word "fulfilled" in the New Testament. "Now all this is come to pass, that it might be fulfilled which was spoken by the Lord through the prophet . . ." (Matt. 1:22; cf. 2:5, 15, 17, 23; 3:3; 4:14, *et al.*). The early parts of the Bible were written in the expectation of someone (Christ) and something (the kingdom of Christ) yet to come. The later parts were written in the confidence that all things were now being brought to fruition. "Concerning which salvation the prophets sought and searched diligently, who prophesied of the grace that should come unto you: searching what time or what manner of time the Spirit of Christ which was in them did point unto, when it testified beforehand the sufferings of Christ, and the glories that should follow them. To whom it was revealed, that not unto themselves, but unto you, did they minister these things, which now have been announced unto you through them that preached the gospel unto you by the Holy Spirit sent forth from heaven; which things angels desire to look into." (1 Pet. 1:10-12).

As Hugo McCord has written:

> Stories begun in one portion of the Bible, left incomplete, are brought to a conclusion in the last book. The story of the tree of life, last mentioned early in the divine record, is finished by John in Revelation. The story of pain and tears, begun with the first mother, is climaxed by the removal of every tear. The story of curses, begun with the first sin, is completed with the divine assurance "there shall be no curse any more." The history of sacrifices, started soon after the expulsion from Eden, is brought to a thrilling climax in Revelation's story of the Lion of Judah who looked like a lamb who had been slain.[2]

"In its structure the Bible is a unit, each part interlaced with and interpreted by other parts, so that every part is necessary to a complete understanding of the whole."[3] This unity of structure could not have come about by accident.

Unity of Teaching About Christ

The unity of Scripture can be convincingly demonstrated by tracing any single teaching or doctrine from Genesis to Revelation. For example, the doctrine of man is totally coherent in its development in the Bible. His origin, fall, redemption and destiny are treated by numerous writers of both Old and New Testaments with complete harmony. Or one might study the church—beginning with the prophecies given in the Old Testament and in the first four books of the New Testament and continuing through the history of its establishment and spread—and see the beautiful wholeness and unity which manifests itself so prominently.

The Bible is not written as a textbook of *systematic theology* with all its teachings on a single subject grouped together. But when the Bible is studied systematically and when its teachings are gathered by subjects, one discerns a unity which would have been humanly impossible to produce.

Surely the best example of this unity of doctrine in Scripture has to do with its teaching concerning Jesus Christ. In prophecy and in fulfillment, the Bible speaks with one voice of him who is presented therein as Savior and Lord. "The study of all that concerns Him throughout the Scriptures, in the law of Moses, the Prophets, the Psalms (Luke 24:47, 44) and the New Testament, convinces one of the unity of the Bible, in such a way that he can never doubt it again."[4]

Immediately after the sin of Adam and Eve, God promised that a Savior would come of the seed of the woman and crush the head (i.e., power) of Satan. (Gen. 3:15; cf. Gal. 4:4). The prophets uniformly testified that this Savior would be born of the tribe of Judah. (Gen. 49:10; Mic. 5:2; cf. Heb. 7:14). Moreover, it was predicted that he would come from the royal line of David. (Isa. 9:7; 11:1; cf. Matt. 1:1). He was to be born in Bethlehem (Mic. 5:2; cf. Matt. 2:1) and his mother was to be a virgin. (Isa. 7:14; cf. Matt. 1:18). He was to have a forerunner who would come in the spirit of Elijah. (Mal. 3:1; 4:5; cf. Luke 1:17). He was to suffer in silence at the hands of his enemies. (Isa. 53:7; cf. Mk. 15:3-5). His bones were not to be broken in his death. (Psa. 24:20; cf. John 20:32-33, 36). Gentiles were to be given access to God's grace by means of his death. (Hos. 2:23; cf. Eph. 2:14-16). The Savior was to be raised from the dead. (Psa. 16:10; John 1:17; cf. Acts 2:32).

These represent but a few examples of the totally harmonious doctrine of Christ which is contained in Scripture. And there is not a single contradiction to be found! Skeptics and unbelievers have searched in vain for just one discrepancy to parade before Christians! If one man had written all these things on the same day and carefully checked against all possibility of self-contradiction, the unity could not be greater than that which we actually find!

Conclusion

If one were to assemble forty historians and ask them to write individual papers on "The Principal Causes of World War I," he would naturally expect disagreement. One author might emphasize the economic issues which helped to bring about exploitation, friction between governments and, finally, outbreaks of fighting. Another man might give primary emphasis to sociological factors which preceded the outbreak of war. Still another might concentrate entirely on political leaders and their decisions which led to the actual breach of the peace. Or it might be that five of the historians would write on the political figures who were most directly involved in the war, yet each of the five might interpret each man's role differently from the other writers! It is practically impossible to get forty men to write on any subject with unanimous sentiment!

But the forty men who helped in the writing of the Bible wrote with complete agreement with each other. And there is no subject in the world which is more controversial than religion! Yes, the Bible is unique in all the world! It is from God!

In closing this brief section on the unity of Scripture, consider this well-worded statement from a French author:

> To what can one attribute this unity running through the whole Bible: unity of vision, structure, message and doctrine—in spite of the long centuries and the many individuals used as instruments for its completion? To this question there can be only one answer: in reality, Scripture has but one Author, the Holy Spirit. To Him, it is but one revelation, since he speaks throughout of the only true and proper Object of worship. There is just one salvation: announced, then effected and consummated by one only Saviour. Human nature is the same through all the ages: its needs, weaknesses

and potential will always require this same divine communication. For the ever-living, omniscient God, time is as one instant; in other words, eternity means an eternal present, from the first page of Scripture to the last. Finally, truth itself is "one" and could never be contradictory.[5]

CHAPTER V

The Scientific Accuracy of the Bible as Proof of Its Inspiration

The Bible is not a textbook on science and is not designed to unlock all the mysteries of the physical universe to mankind. But this is not to say that the Bible is *unscientific* or *incorrect* in any of its statements bearing on scientific matters. If all Scripture is "God-breathed" and if every statement in it was produced only as men "were moved by the Holy Spirit," then any sort of error within it would be traceable to God. If God created the universe and all things within it, should he not understand his creation and be capable of speaking accurately concerning it? A single error of any type—whether in relation to science or any other subject—would negate the Bible's claim to be from an omniscient God.

In every instance where a statement is made in the Bible relative to any scientific matter, the Bible is unfailingly accurate. In spite of the fact that its various parts were written in times of scientific backwardness, there is not a single error in the Word of God! To be sure, the language is popular and not technical. Thus Scripture is found to contain such figurative expressions as sunrise and sunset. We know that the sun does not actually rise and set in relation to the earth. The earth rotates on its axis. But we still use such figurative expressions as this in our ordinary conversations—even though we live in a "scientific" world.

Beyond this, the Bible anticipates many discoveries of science which were made long after the original statements were set down in Scripture. Several examples of this will be cited in the course of this chapter.

The Alleged "Conflict" Between Science and Scripture

Many people have been led to believe that the Bible is filled with myths and errors about scientific matters. It is sad that young people have been told to choose between an ancient book filled with absurd and fanciful tales and the modern-day passion for truth which is characteristic of science.

It simply is not true that the proven facts of science disprove the Bible. To the contrary, it can be demonstrated that true science and the Bible are fully complementary to each other. No "conflict" exists between the two. The *apparent* conflict stems from misguided students who would make the Bible say things it does not say or from scientists who draw conclusions which are unjustified by the data at hand. It would therefore be correct to say that some Bible students and some scientists have been in conflict. But it would be terribly incorrect to say that the Bible and science are in conflict!

Notice an example of a case where an ignorance of the Bible creates an apparent conflict between it and science. There are countless individuals who honestly believe that the creation of the world took place in 4004 B.C. Yet the evidence available to scientists points to a very old earth, possibly several billion years old. A seventeenth-century archbishop of the Roman Catholic Church calculated 4004 B.C. as the date of the earth's creation. Since he was a religious official, people believed him correct and many publishers still print Archbishop Ussher's date in the margins of Bibles. The Bible simply says: "In the beginning God created the heavens and the earth." (Gen. 1:1). The "beginning" could have been millions or billions of years ago. Or it could have been only a few thousand years ago—with the earth having been "aged" at the time God brought it into existence. We just do not know when the creation of this planet occurred! The Bible does not tell us and scientific theories differ greatly. Is there a conflict between the Bible and science here? No. The conflict is between a *theory* advanced by a seventeenth-century theologian and certain *theories* advanced by modern-day scientists.

Now let us take an example of a case wherein unjustified conclusions drawn by certain scientists have created an apparent conflict between science and the Bible. Since Charles Darwin advanced his *theory* of the evolutionary origin of man, men have come more and more to treat that theory as established fact—which it is not! If evolution were a matter of established fact, there would be a conflict between science and the Bible. The truth is that the more men learn in the fields of genetics and related biological sciences the less credible the theory of evolution becomes! Evolution is not scientifically demonstrable and represents a philosophic interpretation of certain data. Such "interpretations" do not have the weight of the facts themselves.

Science and the Bible are not in conflict. False Biblical interpretation and false interpretation of scientific data are frequently in conflict, but the established *facts* of the two disciplines are complementary to each other rather than contradictory! The Christian need not feel embarrassed to stand his ground and affirm his absolute confidence in the Biblical record!

The Bible gives its sanction to the work of science. After God had created the first pair of human beings, he spoke to them and said, "Be fruitful, and multiply, and replenish the earth, and subdue it; and have dominion over the fish of the sea, and over the birds of the heavens, and over every living thing that moveth upon the earth." (Gen. 1:28). Here, at the very beginning of man's existence, is authorization from God to observe, study, experiment with and subdue his physical surroundings. Here is the first call to scientific pursuit! And the call is from God rather than Satan. There is nothing evil about science. It is rooted in this commission from God.

The Bible has nothing to fear from scientific inquiry. It is only further substantiated by every discovery of truth.

STATEMENT OF ARGUMENT

The scientific accuracy of the Bible is an amazing phenomenon. It is a powerful argument for the Bible's supernatural origin, for mere mortals drawing upon the most advanced "science" of their times could not have produced such a book as this in ancient times.

The logical formulation of the basic argument to be developed in this chapter is as follows:

(1) If the particular characteristics of the Bible's treatment of science transcend mere human invention, then the Bible is of divine origin.
(2) The particular characteristics of the Bible's treatment of science do transcend mere human invention.
(3) Therefore the Bible is of divine origin.

MISTAKES THE BIBLE DOES NOT MAKE

In order to explain a point which was hinted at in the introduction to this chapter, let us begin our study of the scientific accuracy of the Bible with a negative observation. The Bible is truly remarkable for the things it *does not say* about our world and life within it. For example, the Egyptians thought the earth was supported by five great pillars. In spite of the fact that Moses was brought up by Pharaoh's daughter and trained in the "learning" of Egyptian "scientists," one does not find any trace of this unscientific notion in his writings. The ideas of a flat earth, the spontaneous generation of life, Ptolemaic astronomy and countless other errors of antiquity are not contained in the Bible.

> The Bible does not avoid these mistakes by failing to deal with a variety of subjects or dealing in ambiguous statements. Rather it covers a wide range of subjects on which learned men have erred

and deals boldly and emphatically with those considered. Other books which have dealt with these subjects in this fashion have one notable thing in common. They contain mistakes.[1]

When all other books of antiquity are examined, whole hosts of errors concerning scientific matters leap from their pages. But the Bible is different. It contains not one single error. It is scientifically accurate to the most minute detail! It is God's Word and therefore pure and without error!

Harry Rimmer and the Research Science Bureau offered $1,000 reward to anyone "finding and proving a scientific error in the Scriptures." One man claimed the money and went to court to prove a certain miracle of the Bible a scientific impossibility. He lost his case! Neither did anyone else ever succeed in claiming the money!

EXAMPLES OF SCIENTIFIC ACCURACY

From a positive point of view, it can be demonstrated that the Bible displays a marvelous precision in all its scientific statements. And in those places where the Bible differs from the "scientific" theories of the time in which it was originally written, it is the Bible which has been shown to be correct by the later discoveries of more enlightened students of the physical world.

First, consider that all living things reproduce only "after their kind." This scientific principle is treated ten times in the opening chapter of the Bible. Now at the time Moses wrote this, people of the "scientific" community would not have agreed with him. In fact, it was not until the days of Pasteur and Lister that scientists knew that worms and insects did not arise by spontaneous generation.

Those who hold to the *theory* of evolution today are forced to contend that one kind of living creature can give rise to an altogether different one. But the facts are conclusively against this. While there are many sizes, colors and types of dogs—Saint Bernard, Chihuahua, Greyhound, etc.—they are all still dogs. Dogs never give birth to kittens, canaries, horses or humans! Living things reproduce only "after their kind." Any reputable scientist will admit that insofar as the *proven* and *observable* facts of science are concerned (not some *theory* which would demand exceptions to our factual information), plants and animals do indeed reproduce only "after their kind."

Second, the Bible asserts a scientific fact about the significance of blood to human life. "But flesh with the life thereof, which is the blood thereof, shall ye not eat." (Gen. 9:4). This same truth is stated twice in the book of Leviticus. "For the life of the flesh is in the blood . . . For as to the life of all flesh, the blood thereof is all one with the life thereof." (Lev. 17:11, 14).

Men did not understand the important role of the blood and its circulatory system until only recent times. It was in the early 1600s that William Harvey advanced the theory of the blood's circulation through the body. It has been far closer to our own time that scientists learned that blood carries oxygen and nutrients to every cell of the body, that it collects and discharges carbon dioxide and other wastes from human tissues, that its white corpuscles fight infections and so on. The Bible asserted that "the life of the flesh is in the blood" long before science learned it was true!

As recently as the time of George Washington, physicians who did not understand the important role of the blood thought "bleeding" a patient would rid his body of impurities and restore his health. Now we know that this was a foolish treatment, for it weakens the body by draining away its life-giving fluid! The Bible anticipated the recent discovery that life is in the blood!

Third, the amazing character of certain Old Testament instructions concerning hygiene, sanitation and quarantine clearly were unique for their time and anticipated many modern discoveries. For example, present-day textbooks on leprosy refer to the remarkable passages relating to the diagnosis and prevention of leprosy in Leviticus.[2] Many valid sanitary precautions against the spread of communicable diseases are found in Leviticus 13. The burial of human waste outside the camp (cf. Deut. 23:12-13) had an obvious advantage to the health of the people.[3]

> There is no doubt that the medical practices of the Jews of Moses' day were far advanced beyond

those of neighboring nations. In many respects Hebrew medical practices were thousands of years ahead of their times. Moses was trained in all the ways of the Egyptians (Acts 7:22) and this most certainly included training in Egyptian medical practices. Nevertheless, one finds that the Pentateuch is free of Egyptian superstitious medical beliefs and, in most instances, Hebrew medical practices far excelled those of the Egyptians. For example, the *Papyrus Ebers*, a medical book written in Egypt about the time of Moses suggested drug remedies containing such bizarre items as the fat of a hippopotamus, crocodile, cat or snake, the hoof of a donkey, heads of worms, brains of fishes and tadpoles, and excreta from donkeys, antelopes, dogs, cats, flies, and human beings.[4]

While one must remember that these rules and regulations were given to the Israelites in a religious context as tests of faith, the fact remains that they reflect scientifically accurate principles and practices.

It is entirely immaterial whether the hygiene and prophylaxis as promulgated by Moses in the Pentateuch were intended as religious rituals or as health measures. The fact is they were scientifically sound . . . The fact is that neither the Old Egyptian medical documents nor other early medical codes have been so thoroughgoing on subjects of hygiene and prophylaxis as the Mosaic Code.[5]

Fourth, the Bible correctly states that the earth is circular in shape (not flat) and has no visible means of support. These facts are indisputably asserted in Isaiah 40:22 and Job 26:7.

Fifth, the Bible says that the stars cannot be counted for their multitude. (Cf. Gen. 15:5; 22:17). Ancient people thought there were but a few hundred stars and that they could be numbered. Hipparchus, in the second century before Christ, set the number at 1,080. Two centuries after Christ, Ptolemy set the number at 1,025. Today, with powerful telescopes that have discovered whole galaxies of stars beyond our own, we know that the Bible was scientifically accurate in its assertion.

On and on this listing could go: the paths in the seas (Psa. 8:8; Isa. 40:16), the chemical composition of the physical body (Gen. 2:7), etc. But these few demonstrations of the scientific accuracy of the Bible must suffice for this brief chapter.

Conclusion

This Bible is not a "child of its times." It is not marred by the crude errors of ancient "science." And the only possible explanation of this fact is that the Bible is from God, not mere men.

CHAPTER VI

The Uniqueness of the Biblical View of Things as an Evidence of Inspiration

Do not let the title of this chapter confuse or mislead you. The theme to be expanded in this section is simply difficult to state in the form of a concise title! A few words of explanation are therefore in order at the beginning.

Colleges and universities across the country offer courses in *comparative religions.* The thesis of such courses is that Christianity is not distinctive and unique but is merely a variation on the basic themes running through all the world religions. In other words, the Muslim, Buddhist or Hindu is said to worship the same God we do—only under a different name and in some different but not inferior methods. Is this true? Does the study of comparative religions show that other religions are as noble and worthy of acceptance as Christianity?

In particular, someone might ask, "Since there are 'sacred books' other than the Bible, how can anyone assume that the Bible alone is true and all the others are false?

Are not all the so-called 'sacred books' very much alike and on the same general level?"

In comparison to the general run of ideas found in non-Biblical religions, the religious concepts set forth in the Bible stand out like a majestic mountain peak! The Bible's view of God and man in relation to God is so obviously superior to that presented by any other religion as to be incapable of proper comparison. The Bible shows itself to be a *divine production* as contrasted to the purely *human productions* which are passed off as "sacred books" in other religions!

The manifest excellence of the Bible's view of things over that found in other religions and their books serves to confirm and further establish one's faith in the Bible as deity's one and only book of revelation. Stated in precise logical form, the argument of this chapter is as follows:

(1) If the great doctrines of the Bible (e.g., God, creation, man, sin and salvation) are of such nature as to be incapable of human origin, then the Bible must be traced to a superhuman (i.e., divine) source and be regarded as the very Word of God.

(2) The great doctrines of the Bible (e.g., God, creation, man, sin and salvation) are of such nature as to be incapable of human origin.

(3) Therefore the Bible must be traced to a superhuman (i.e., divine) source and be regarded as the very Word of God.

For the sake of demonstrating the general superiority which characterizes the Bible's view of things, take careful note of the things discussed in this chapter.

THE BIBLE'S DOCTRINE OF GOD

If the thesis of comparative religions that all religious systems are essentially alike is true, one should certainly be able to discern agreement with regard to the fundamental doctrine of God. Such is definitely not the case!

Does the God, god or gods presented by other religions correspond to the infinite, personal, intelligent and moral God who is presented in the Bible as creator and sustainer of the entire visible universe? No, this God is found only in the Bible! He is not a local god who is interested in only a few of the world's people; he is the creator of the heavens and the earth and all that is in them and is motivated by love to seek the welfare of all humanity. He is not a sensual god who gives way to such base emotions as envy and revenge; he is perfect in holiness and punishes sin justly, not with delight but with grief. He is not capricious in his actions; he acts purposefully so as to achieve his righteous will among his creatures. In no age and in no civilization of history have mere mortals attributed such noble and perfect qualities to their god or gods. The concept of such a God as the Bible sets forth is simply beyond human invention!

Buddha, contrary to popular belief, never claimed to be deity. In fact, he was agnostic about the whole question of whether God even existed. If God existed, the Buddha taught emphatically, he could not help an individual achieve enlightenment. Each person must work this out for himself.

Hindus are pantheistic. *Pan* means "all" and *theistic* means "God." Hindus believe that God and the universe are identical. The concept of "maya" is central to their thinking. Maya means that the material world is an illusion and that reality is spiritual and invisible. Brahm is the impersonal, all-pervading force of the universe, and the ultimate goal is for man to be reunited with this "God" in nirvana. Buddhism also teaches that the material world is an illusion. It is readily apparent why modern science came to birth through Christians, who believed in a personal God and an orderly universe, rather than in the context of Oriental philosophy. It is clear why most scientific progress has come from the West rather than the East. Why would one investigate what he believes is an illusion? In Islam and Judaism we have a God much closer to the Christian concept. Here God is personal and transcendant, or separate from his creation. Surely, we are urged, we may get together with those who believe in God in personal terms.

But as we examine the Muslim concept of God—"Allah," as he is called in the *Koran*—we find he is not the God and Father of Jesus Christ, but rather, as in all other instances, a God of man's own imagination. Our knowledge of Allah comes from the

Koran, which came t h r o u g h Mohammed. Mohammed, like Buddha and unlike Jesus Christ, did not claim deity. He taught that he was only the prophet of Allah. The picture of God which comes through to us in the pages of the Koran is one who is totally removed from men, one who is capricious in all of his acts, responsible for evil as well as for good, and certainly not the God who "so loved the world that he gave his only begotten Son, that whoever believes in him should not perish but have eternal life." (John 3:16). It is this totally distant concept of God that makes the idea of his becoming man utterly inconceivable to the Muslim. How could their god, so majestic and beyond reach, have contact with mortal man in sin and misery? The death of God the Son on the cross is likewise inconceivable to a Muslim, since this would mean God was defeated by his creatures—an impossibility to the Muslim.

The Jewish concept of God is closest of all to the Christian. Isn't the God whom they worship the God of the Old Testament, which the Christian accepts? Surely they can get together on this!

Again, however, closer examination shows that the Jews would not admit their God was the Father of Jesus Christ. In fact, it was this very issue that precipitated such bitter controversy in Jesus' time. We accept God, they said to Christ, but we do not accept you because as a man you make yourself God, which is blasphemy.

In a conversation with the Jews, Christ discussed this question. "God is our Father," they said. Jesus said to them, "If God were your Father, you would love me, for I proceeded and came forth from God . . . He who is of God hears the words of God; the reason why you do not hear them is that you are not of God" (John 8:42, 47). In even stronger words he says, "You are of your father the devil." (v. 44).[1]

Biblical truth about God is not only unique but is also *exclusive*. The worship of gods other than the one true and living God is sin! (Cf. Deut. 32:17; 1 Cor. 10:20).

Only the Biblical view of God is a sound and reasonable view. This view could not have been conceived by unaided human intelligence. It came by special revelation in the inspired and infallible Word of God.

THE BIBLE'S DOCTRINE OF CREATION

The Bible's view of origins is also unique. Men of every generation have attempted to explain the origin of the universe and life within it. Their attempts have been amusing, fanciful and ridiculous! Not one of these ancient efforts has any serious proponents and defenders today. But the Biblical account of creation is both sublime and scientific in nature. Many scientists of our day accept this account of origins and unashamedly defend it against its chief modern-day alternative, the theory of evolution.

The book of Genesis opens with these words: "In the beginning God created the heavens and the earth." (Gen. 1:1). This was not the accepted cosmogony (i.e., theory of the origin of the universe) of the time of Moses. The concept of creation by an omnipotent God who called the entire universe into being by his word found its way into Scripture not by human wisdom but by divine revelation!

To show the superiority of this view over other ancient notions of origins, consider the Babylonian story of creation. Some ancient clay tablets found in excavations at Nineveh contain an account of origins known as the "Enuma Elish." These tablets are thought to date back to a period in history somewhat earlier than the time of Moses.

The Enuma Elish tells of a fierce battle between the Babylonian city god, Marduk, and a female god, Tiamat. "Tiamat and Marduk, the wisest of the gods, took their stands opposite each other. They pressed to battle and drew near in combat. He shot off an arrow. It tore her belly, it cut through her vitals. It pierced [her] heart. He split her open like a mussel into two parts; half of her he set in place and formed the sky . . . and a great structure, its counterpart, he established Esharra (the earth) . . ." The story continues by telling that the commander of Tiamat's army, Kingu, was slain. Marduk then commanded his father, Ea, to use Kingu's blood to create man. "They bound him (Kingu) and held him in prison before Ea; they inflicted punishment upon him by cutting open [the arteries of] his blood. With his blood they fashioned mankind . . . After Ea, the wise, had created man and had imposed the service of the gods upon him, that work was past understanding." A great feast was held in honor of Marduk who eventually rose to supremacy over all the other gods.

The difference between the Bible's doctrine of creation and the Enuma Elish are evident. Genesis has no polytheism with gods who envy, hate and kill each other. It says nothing of creating heaven and earth from separate halves of a dead body. Whereas the Babylonian creation myth declares matter to be eternal and makes its gods in man's image, the Bible account of creation presents God as the infinite spirit being who created matter out of nothing and made man in his image. Scholars are in general agreement that the Enuma Elish is a piece of political propaganda designed to advance the cause of Babylon in a bid for supremacy in the Mesopotamian world.

Whatever similarities may be seen in these two accounts of creation are seen to be greatly outweighed by vast differences between them.

The most widely held alternative to the Biblical account of creation in our day is the theory of evolution. From elementary grades through college years, young people are taught that evolution is scientific fact and creation is unscientific myth. Such a contention grossly misrepresents the facts of the case.

First, the theory of evolution is *only a THEORY* and should be so presented. By the very nature of the case, it can never become a fact of science, for the scientific method requires demonstration before a *theory* can be promoted to the level of *fact*. Evolution can never be demonstrated. In fact, one of the most embarrassing things to the evolutionist is that the process which is supposed to have been going on for billions of years has now stopped! There are no in-between forms around us today that are on their way to becoming something better!

Second, it is the theory of evolution and not the Biblical account of creation which is *unscientific* in nature. Whereas this theory holds that things are ever going from the simpler to the more complex and orderly state, observation of nature shows the exact opposite to be true. Wood rots, iron rusts, living things grow old and die. The second law of thermodynamics, which is universally accepted by scientists, says that energy deteriorates as it changes forms. It does not build itself up.

Again, the theory of evolution is unscientific because it offers no mechanism capable of producing the constant forward progress it requires. Darwin suggested "survival of the fittest" and the transmission of acquired characteristics as the mechanism of evolution. No scientist holds this theory today. Cut off a dog's tail and its offspring will still have tails, for the acquired traits are not transmitted. Neither are mutations adequate to explain the development of new and superior life forms, for "In more than 99 per cent of cases the mutation of a gene produces some kind of harmful effect, some disturbance of function."[2]

While changes occur within the categories of living things (e.g., there are many varieties of dogs), it is not true that one category, or "kind," of organisms is capable of giving rise to another category (e.g., single-celled organisms giving rise to multi-celled ones). But evolution requires this sort of thing and is therefore unscientific in its nature.

Third, many qualified and respected *scientists are challenging the theory of evolution* solely on the basis of its lack of harmony with available evidence. Dr. John N. Moore, a professor at Michigan State University, addressed a meeting of the American Association for the Advancement of Science in December of 1971 and flatly stated that Darwin's theory of evolution is "more illogical than biological." Dr. Moore pointed out that if life had evolved from a single cell there should be an increase in chromosomes and the quality of the gene material carried by the chromosomes as the complexity of animals increases. He continued, "Absolutely no pattern of increase of chromosome number from less complex to most complex is at all detectable." In fact, Dr. Moore pointed out, exactly the opposite can be shown to be true in certain cases. For example, chromosome counts place man *lower* than frogs and toads, which is contradictory to what the theory of evolution would require to be the case. Dr. Moore stated: "The typical evolutionary explanation doesn't make sense in view of today's knowledge."[3]

Fourth, the Bible account of creation is altogether *sci-*

entific in character (i.e., it does not conflict with a single demonstrable fact of science) and is not to be dismissed as a myth of antiquity. The second law of thermodynamics demands that the universe must have had a time of beginning. If it had always existed, it would have worn itself out by now. The Bible agrees with this and says, "In the beginning God created the heavens and the earth." (Gen. 1:1). Again, in Genesis 1:11-25 it is stated ten times that each living unit of creation would reproduce "after its kind." This is scientific and is supported by all the known facts.

Science can tell us what is going on in the universe now, but it cannot tell us what started these processes into operation. This could be known only by revelation from God. The Bible is just such a revelation and is fully reliable in all matters of history, science, etc. There is not one single demonstrable error anywhere in the Bible.

The widespread acceptance of the evolutionary theory is largely responsible for the disintegration of our society —disintegration witnessed in materialism, immorality, crime, permissiveness, atheism, etc. It will not do to scrap the productive truth of the Bible for the destructive theories of certain philosopher-scientists.

The Bible's Doctrine of Man

The Biblical doctrine of a personal God who created man in his own image gives rise to a unique doctrine of man.

Whereas the evolutionary system makes man a mere graduate beast, the Bible presents man as being created above the animals and having dominion over them. (Gen. 1:24-31). Man bears the image of his Creator in that he has self-consciousness, emotions, intellect and will. He is of infinite worth because his spirit is immortal. He is loved of God.

Each individual is not only to view himself in this light but is also to see his neighbor as he sees himself. This means that no person or race has the right to consider itself better than another. The notion of racial superiority seems to be so common in the world and certain religions actually foster this spirit. The Bible does not give support to it but rather refutes it. (Note: God's selection of the Jews to bring the Messiah into the world did not indicate racial superiority. Futhermore, the Jews were specifically warned not to consider themselves better than others. Cf. Deut. 7:7-8; Ex. 22:21; Lev. 19:33-34).

The Bible declares that God created all men and desires their worship and service in this life and their fellowship in the life to come. "Of a truth I perceive that God is no respecter of persons: but in every nation he that feareth him, and worketh righteousness, is acceptable to him." (Acts 10:34b-35).

How did the Bible come to contain this unique, exalted and elevating doctrine of man? It came not by human invention but by divine revelation.

The Bible's Doctrine of Sin and Salvation

Although the Bible shows man's nobility of origin and purpose, it also presents him as a sinner in need of salvation. Man was created with freedom of will—this was necessary if he was to be in the image of God and not a mere robot. But this freedom has been generally used to choose and perform selfish, unloving and unrighteous deeds. We did not have to sin, but we did. And having sinned there was no way for us to save ourselves. Only love and grace from the infinite God who provided Jesus Christ as our vicarious substitute could save us from death!

Non-Biblical religions consistently picture men as taking the initiative to seek after their deity and struggle for his favor. The Bible alone shows God as taking the initiative in seeking after man. The difference in these two concepts is a profound one.

> What salvation is, and what we are pointing toward, is quite different in the world's religions from what it is in Christianity.
>
> In Buddhism, for instance, the ultimate goal is nirvana, or the extinction of desire. According to Buddha's teaching, all pain and suffering come from desire. If this desire can be overcome by following the Eightfold Path to Enlightenment, one can

achieve nirvana, which is total nothingness. It is likened to the snuffing out of a candle. This is what is supposed to happen to life and consciousness when nirvana has been achieved.

In Hinduism the ultimate goal is also nirvana, but the term here has a different meaning. Nirvana is ultimate reunion with Brahm, the all-pervading force of the universe which is the Hindu's god. This experience is likened to the return of a drop of water to the ocean. Individuality is lost in the reunion with "God," but without the total self-annihilation of Buddhism. Nirvana, in Hindusim, is achieved through a continuous cycle of birth, life, death, and rebirth. As soon as any animal, insect, or human being dies, it or he is immediately reborn in another form. Whether one moves up or down the scale of life depends on the quality of moral life one has lived. If it has been a good life, one moves up the scale with more comfort and less suffering. If one has lived a bad life, he moves down the scale into suffering and poverty. If he has been bad enough he is not reborn as a human being at all, but as an animal or insect. This law of reaping in the next life, the harvest of one's present life is called the law of Karma. It explains why Hindus will not kill even an insect, not to mention a sacred cow, though these inhibitions pose grave sanitation and public health problems. What seems strange, curious, and even ludicrous to us of the western world has a very clear rationale to the Hindu, and to us once we understand his thinking.

In Islam, heaven is a paradise of wine, women and song. It is achieved by living a life in which, ironically, one abstains from the things he will be rewarded with in paradise. In addition to this abstention, one must follow the Five Pillars of Islam: repeating the creed, making a pilgrimage to Mecca, giving alms to the poor, praying five times daily, and keeping the fast of the month of Ramadan.[4]

Pagan religion leaves the human soul in darkness and with an aching void. It drives its devotees with fear and superstition.

It makes man responsible for saving himself and thus leaves him utterly without and incapable of assurance and confidence. Biblical religion brings one to Jesus Christ where there is light, knowledge, joy and confidence.

It shows us salvation which depends not on our ability to accomplish but only on our willingness to accept a free gift!

This concept of sin and its remedy is not of human invention. In the very nature of the case, it is beyond human invention.

Conclusion

Nowhere in any of the non-Biblical religions is there anything resembling the profound, reasonable and sublime doctrinal content of the Holy Scritpures. "Since unaided human beings outside the Bible have not produced such great doctrines as set forth in the Scriptures concerning God, concerning man's nature, and concerning man's duty, strong indication exists that unaided human beings could not originate those great doctrines. Those great doctrines therefore are internal attestations to the superhuman origin of the Bible."[5]

CHAPTER VII

The Testimony of Archaeology to the Trustworthiness of the Bible

The point has been made earlier in this book that the case for Biblical inspiration and authority must be made from the Bible itself. By its very content and nature, the Bible must show itself to be of supernatural origin. It must unquestionably be a book which human wisdom could not have produced. Evidence to the effect that the Bible must be seen as such a book has been presented in the forms of predictive prophecy, a humanly inexplicable unity, total accuracy and even anticipation of discoveries in science, and a world view which cannot be accounted for on the basis of human invention. These traits absolutely require us to look for a supernatural origin for the Bible. Only God could have produced such a book!

In addition to the Bible's *internal* evidences of inspiration, there are numerous *external* confirmations of its complete trustworthiness. Among these are geography, history, archaeology, and others. This chapter will give brief attention to the weighty testimony of archaeology to the accuracy and reliability of the Word of God.

The Place of Archaeology

From the beginning of this study, let it be clearly understood that external evidences are confirmatory in their nature rather than of primary significance in establishing the inspiration and authority of Scripture. External evidences can demonstrate the factuality of the Biblical record in the light of various sciences; but this does not of itself prove inspiration. Whereas an inspired book would necessarily be historically and geographically accurate, other books might meet these tests and still be uninspired. To repeat an example cited earlier, a carefully documented history of the United States might conform to the facts without error but the man who wrote it would not have been guided by the Holy Spirit.

> The ground of faith in Scripture as the Word of God is therefore the evidence it inherently contains of its divine authorship and quality. External evidence, witness to its divinity derived from other sources extraneous to itself, may corroborate and confirm the witness it inherently contains, but such external evidence cannot be in the category of evidence sufficient to ground and constrain faith . . . Faith in Scripture as God's Word, then, rests upon the perfections inherent in Scripture and is elicited by the perception of these perfections.[1]

What, then, is the value of archaeology in relation to apologetics? Archaeology serves to confirm the credibility of the individual writers of both the Old and New Testaments and, as a result, gives testimony to their integrity when they claim to speak with divine authority about the nature of God or the requirements for salvation. If archaeology, on the other hand, shows that the Bible errs in many places, how can we have confidence in its general reliability?

Perhaps an illustration will help clarify this point. A witness on the stand in a particular criminal case is giving crucial testimony. His testimony consists, let us say, of ten interrelated facts. If eight of those facts can be corroborated by evidence introduced independent of the man testifying and if the other two facts cannot be controverted, the judge and jury will likely consider him a credible witness and accept his testimony as completely true. But if two or three of his facts which can be checked by other evidence are shown to be in error, the totality of his testimony is discredited. By the same token, if the statements of the Bible which are capable of being checked are corroborated by independent evidence and if none of its statements can be controverted, any reasonable and fair-minded man will be disposed to accept its total testimony. This is the essential value of archaeology to the study of apologetics.

Dr. Joseph P. Free has correctly observed:

> The Bible is a historical book, and the great truths of Christianity are founded upon the historic facts revealed therein. If the fact of the Virgin Birth, the fact of the Crucifixion, and the fact of the Resurrection be set aside, our faith is without foundation. Since the New Testament revelation stands upon the foundation of the Old Testament, the accuracy of the Old Testament is of great importance to us. The accuracy and historicity of the Scriptures has been denied by the destructive critic, who has set aside the full validity of the Bible at point after point. For example, certain critics have said that the accounts of Abraham are legendary, that Mosaic legislation was formulated hundreds of years after the time of Moses, that such people as the Hittites were either legendary or insignificant, that the book of Judges was composed of "good stories" and not really historical accounts, that various people ranging from Sargon to Sanballat were unhistorical. Yet archaeological discoveries have shown that these critical charges and countless others are wrong and that the Bible is trustworthy in the very statements which have been set aside as untrustworthy.[2]

William F. Albright, one of the truly great archaeologists of modern times, has had this to say:

The excessive scepticism shown toward the Bible by

59

important historical schools of the eighteenth and nineteenth centuries, certain phases of which still appear periodically, has been progressively discredited. Discovery after discovery has established the accuracy of innumerable details, and has brought increased recognition to the value of the Bible as a source of history.[3]

Archaeology has discovered people, events, and whole civilizations which were known about only from the Bible. Based on the silence of records other than the one in the Scripture, numerous critics argued that the Bible was in error. With the passing of time and the unearthing of more data, the Bible has been repeatedly vindicated and never contradicted. Nelson Glueck, a renowned Jewish archaeologist, has written: "It may be stated categorically that no archaeological discovery has ever controverted a biblical reference."[4] Millar Burrows, of Yale University, says: "Archaeology has in many cases refuted the views of modern critics. It has shown in a number of instances that these views rest on false assumptions and unreal, artificial schemes of historical development."[5] The Bible has never been falsified by the findings of archaeology; its critics have been shown to be in error many times! Which ought men to judge trustworthy?

So much literature is available on the discoveries of archaeology as they pertain to the Bible that no extensive listing of these important matters is either possible or desirable in a book of this type. For the purposes of illustration and elementary appreciation of the contributions of archaeology, three examples have been selected which relate to the Old Testament and three which relate to the New Testament.

ARCHAEOLOGY AND THE OLD TESTAMENT

With reference to the Old Testament, consider first the history of the patriarchal period and especially those parts relating to Abraham. Writing before the recent finds of archaeology, the nineteenth-century critical scholar who did so much to overthrow confidence in the reliability of the Old Testament records, Julius Wellhausen, said: "We attain to no historical knowledge of the patriarchs, but only of the time when the stories about them arose in the Israelite people; this latter age is here unconsciously projected, in its inner and its outward features, into hoary antiquity, and is reflected there like a glorified image."[6] The passing of time and the research of archaeologists since Wellhausen's time have produced irrefutable evidence which shows that the lives of the patriarchs fit into history precisely where the Bible had placed them!

For a long time—and the notion still persists in some circles—it was insisted that the camel was unknown to the Near East in the days of the patriarchs. Thus it was alleged that the Bible's writers were projecting backward into history certain conditions of their much later times. Statuettes, carvings, and even bones of the camel have now been found in Egypt which date back at least as far as 3000 B.C.!

In the light of extensive literature (i.e., clay tablets) and other data recovered from excavations at Nuzi and Mari, we know that the social and cultural conditions reflected in the Scripture are accurate for the periods covered.

Abraham was no mythical "cult-hero of the Hebrew religion." He was a real man who lived under the circumstances related in the ancient Biblical record. "Everything indicates that here we have an historical individual. As noted above, he is not mentioned in any known archaeological source, but his name appears in Babylonia as a personal name in the very period to which he belongs."[7]

One last observation in this regard has to do with the Old Testament record of the fact that a brass laver for the tabernacle was said to have been fashioned of brass which had been obtained from the mirrors of the women. (Cf. Ex. 38:8). Julius Wellhausen, mentioned earlier as a critic of the Bible's reliability, argued that bronze mirrors were unknown in Egypt and its surrounding areas at the early date the Bible indicates. He thus reasoned that such a reference was an addition from a much later time, possibly around 500 B.C. The findings of archaeology have altogether discredited this sort of reasoning. "There is specific archaeological evidence showing the use of such bronze mirrors in the Empire Period of Egyptian history

(c. 1500-1200 B.C.). This period is contemporary with Moses and the Exodus from Egypt. The excavations in Egypt have brought forth many bronze mirrors..."[8]

Second, archaeology has verified the Scripture's account of the wealth and grandeur of King Solomon. Critics of the Word of God had long cast doubt on First Kings and the assertions it makes: that Solomon had a navy (9:26), that he had a vast number of horses and chariots (10:26), that he was a great builder who had access to equipment for the refining of metal (7-8), etc. How could the king of little, insignificant Palestine have attained unto such wealth and power as the Bible indicates for him? Surely, the critics indicated, it was easy to see that these were embellishments of fact and even outright myths in many cases!

Digs have been conducted into the ruins of cities which prospered in Solomon's time and the evidence has shown that the Biblical record is perfectly harmonious with historical data. The excavation of Megiddo revealed a huge stable—a structure large enough to house several hundred horses. Some of the stone mangers and hitching posts are still in place. Nearby were the barracks of Solomon's chariot battalions. Similar structures have been found at Hazor, Taanach, and Jerusalem.

What of Solomon's navy? "It is apparent too that construction of a seaport on the Gulf of Aqabah and of a navy for Solomon (1 Kings 9:26-27) was made possible by technical help from Tyre. A Phoenician priest specifically mentions, in a contemporary document, the building of a fleet of ten ships and names the Phoenician captains in charge of it."[9]

And what of the unlikely claim that Solomon had metal refining equipment? There is no doubt of it today! Nelson Glueck unearthed Ezion-geber during the period 1938-40 and revealed the greatest smelting furnace yet found in the Near East. This was Solomon's seaport on the Red Sea and was located at just the right spot so as to produce a natural forced draft for the furnace. Copper slag, casting molds and earthenware smelting pots have also been found. Glueck was led to call Ezion-geber "the Pittsburgh of Palestine."

Solomon was not an insignificant king over an insignificant people. He reigned with all the splendor, wealth, and power ascribed to him in the Bible. We have the substantiating evidence outside the Bible to verify this claim.

A third Old Testament assertion which was long disputed but is now verified from external sources has to do with the existence of King Sargon. Isaiah 20:1 is the only mention of Sargon in the Bible and was long the only reference to him in all the world's available historical data. Critics of the trustworthiness of the Bible speculated that there was never any such King in Assyria as Sargon and that his name had been invented by a late Biblical writer to fill in a chronological gap. In 1843 Paul Emile Botta discovered the palace of Sargon at Khorsabad. Among nine thousand feet of pictures and inscriptions in the palace, there are two accounts of the very campaign against Ashdod which is referred to in Isaiah 20. Then, within the last few years, an excavation at Ashdod produced the fragments of a victory stele set up there on the occasion of the victory by one of Sargon's officials!

ARCHAEOLOGY AND THE NEW TESTAMENT

Moving now to the New Testament, critics of the Bible long challenged the validity of Luke's reference to the birth of Christ "when Quirinius was governor of Syria." (Luke 2:2). It was alleged that historical records show that Quirinius held this position between A.D. 6 and 12—far too late to fit Luke's narrative.[10] Archaeological discoveries now offer positive proof that Quirinius was governor of Syria *twice*. Two inscriptions, one found at Antioch in Pisidia and the other in a village near Antioch, show that he was governor at the time of the birth of Christ[11] and that he held the same office again at the later time which had been known about by historians and which had incorrectly been assumed to have been his only governorship.

In this same connection, it is interesting that the critics even challenged the notion of an enrollment (cf. Luke 2:1) being made by the Romans which required citizens to return to their ancestral homes. This, of course, is the reason given in Scripture for Joseph and Mary being in Bethlehem at the time of the birth of Jesus. A number of ancient documents have now been discovered which silence these criticisms forever. It is known that under Augustus the enrollment of taxpayers and the taking of a census was conducted every fourteen years and required that family heads return to their family homes. One such enrollment and census occured around 9-6 B.C.—at the very time that Quirinius was governor of Syria. All of Luke's historical references pertaining to the circumstances surrounding the birth of Christ are correct to the most minute detail!

Second, Luke has been charged with making a serious historical blunder in referring to "Lysanias tetrarch of Abilene" as being contemporary with the beginning of the ministry of John the Baptist in A.D. 27. (Luke 3:1).

> Luke has been charged with a gross error in making Lysanias tetrarch of the Abilene at this time. It is said that he confuses this man with the king Lysanias who ruled this territory previous to B.C. 36 and was murdered in that year. The fact that the one was a king and the other, of whom Luke speaks, a tetrarch, seems to escape the critics, as does also an inscription that has been known for a century, a new and improved copy of which was found on the site of Abila. It refers to the dedication of a temple and has the words "on behalf of the salvation of the Lords Imperial and their whole household" by "Nymphaios, a freedman of Lysanias, the tetrarch." "The Lords Imperial" can be only the emperor Tiberius and Julia, his mother. The latter died in A.D. 29, and thus the time of the inscription must come between A.D. 14 (or 12) and 29. Luke is not in error. He lived close to this time and in all his writings shows himself so exact (1:3) and so thoroughly informed on all points.[12]

Again, is it Luke or the critics who deserve to be judged inaccurate? Surely the archaeological vindications are all on the side of the one as opposed to the others!

Third, Luke has been charged with carelessness and error in Acts with reference to the titles he assigned to certain men. For example, he called the rulers of Thessalonica "politarchs" in Acts 17:6. This term as a designation of civil rulers was long unknown from sources outside the

Bible and was thus judged to be an evidence of Luke's unreliability. Archaeology has again vindicated the accuracy of Luke over his critics. "This term *politarchs* is not found in any classical author, but it is found in some nineteen inscriptions, ranging from the second century B.C. to the third century A.D., as a title of magistrates in Macedonian cities. In five of these inscriptions Thessalonica is the Macedonian city in question . . ."[13]

The historical accuracy of Luke, as he wrote under the control of the Holy Spirit, is powerful in its impact upon the honest mind. Sir William Ramsay is generally held to be one of the greatest archaeologists who ever lived. He received his education in circles which were known for unbelief. He was taught and indeed accepted the notion that the book of Acts was a product of the mid-second century and was unreliable as a document of history. He thus began his archaeological work on the basis of these assumptions. As his work progressed and as he saw that Luke was indeed vindicated by the facts, his attitude underwent a great change.

> . . . I found myself brought into contact with the Book of Acts as an authority for the topography, antiquities and society of Asia Minor. It was gradually borne upon me that in various details the narrative showed marvelous truth. In fact, beginning with a fixed idea that the work was essentially a second century composition, and never relying on its evidence as trustworthy for the first century conditions, I gradually came to find it a useful ally in some obscure and difficult investigations.[14]

THE DEAD SEA SCROLLS

In our brief survey of the bearing of archaeology on Biblical studies, it would be a tremendous oversight to fail to give attention to the Dead Sea Scrolls.

A fifteen-year-old Bedouin boy, searching for a lost goat, threw a stone which landed in a cave and broke a piece of pottery. Attracted by the sound of something breaking, the boy looked inside and saw a number of sealed jars which turned out to be containers for old scrolls. This was in the spring of 1947. The scrolls had not seen the light of day for nearly 1900 years, for they had been carefully sealed and hidden around A.D. 68. As it turned out, the scrolls recovered from this cave (and others nearby) totaled more than five hundred and constitute one of the most exciting scholarly finds of modern times. What is the importance of the scrolls? Although more will be said about them in a later chapter on the transmission of the Bible, a few comments are appropriate at this point.

Before the discovery of these scrolls in 1947, our Hebrew text of the Old Testament was based on manuscripts dating from A.D. 900-1000. The Dead Sea Scrolls are dated between 200 B.C. and A.D. 68. Portions of every Old Testament book except Esther are in the collection, as well as a number of commentaries on the Scripture and various extra-Biblical writings. One of the most important of the scrolls is a complete manuscript of the lengthy book of Isaiah.

Scholars who have studied these materials closely have been amazed at their close agreement with the much later texts they had been accustomed to working with. Most of the variations consist of nothing more substantial than variations in spelling!

Do we have a reliable text of the Old Testament? Can we be sure that the Hebrew text has been faithfully preserved so that it accurately represents what was originally written by the original authors? The archaeological finds at Qumran enable us to answer these questions with a resounding affirmative! We have a dependable text of the Old Testament! As Millar Burrows has written concerning the significance of the scrolls: "The general reader and student of the Bible may be satisfied to note that nothing in all this changes our understanding of the religious teaching of the Bible."[15]

Conclusion

External evidences such as archaeology convince us of the total trustworthiness of the Bible and strengthen our confidence that we are dealing with a book beyond human ability to produce!

CHAPTER VIII

Are There Errors in Scripture?

Is the Bible the final determinant of truth in religion? Is the Bible merely a fallible human witness to the acts of God in history which inevitably contains errors? Is there a mediating position between these two views which allows one to grant the claims of the critics against the Bible's factual accuracy and yet view the Bible as a source of spiritual guidance?

The chaos in American theology today can be traced back to its roots in the rejection of the doctrine of Biblical infallibility. The truth claim implicit in the doctrine of inspiration is the foundation for all theology. As Clark H. Pinnock has observed:

> Only because the Bible embodies objectively true communication about the nature of God, the condition of man, and the provision of his salvation, is it possible to begin the theological task. The question of inspiration is then not the plaything of the theological specialist; it is the eminently practical foundation on which the gospel rests.[1]

The Bible has no ultimate authority over mankind if it is not fully inspired in all of its parts. If it is altogether from men, a book written by theological experts of our own day would be as adequate a guide in matters of faith and practice as one written in antiquity. If parts of the Bible are from men and parts of it from God, then man is left without a basis for deciding between the two so as to know what is unquestionably authoritative as opposed to what is mere speculative opinion.

If the Bible is the written Word of God to man, we should apply ourselves to the meticulous study of the Scripture in order to learn the will of God and then give ourselves in careful obedience and conformity to it. On the other hand, if the Bible is not the one authoritative revelation of the will of God to man, there is no compelling reason why we should bother ourselves with it at all. No meaningful difference would be made after we had learned what it teaches.

Reason for Examining Alleged Errors

Chapter Two of this book set forth the Bible's claims for itself. It was shown that both the Old and New Testaments claim to be God-breathed records of divine events in human history. Beyond that, both testaments claim to constitute a revelation of the significance of these events for mankind. God gave the writers of the individual books both the thoughts and the words which accurately expressed his will. The Bible thus claims to be the Word of God which is both infallibly true and fully authoritative.

Subsequent chapters of this book have presented some (but by no means all) of the positive evidence which supports the Bible's claims for itself. But in order to be fully fair in our study it must be granted that some individuals do assert the presence of demonstrated errors in Scripture. And in order to be honest with our own intellects, we must look at the alleged errors and investigate them to see whether they are real or imagined. In this chapter attention will be given to this problem in a general way. In the next two chapters, a number of alleged errors in the Old and New Testaments will be examined. While it will be seen that the Bible contains some *difficult* passages (as does every book), it will become apparent to the fair-minded student that not even one proven error is contained in its pages.

Error Versus Perfection

In recognition of human frailties, men sometimes have no defense for certain mistakes they make except to say, "To err is human." It is indeed the case that human efforts are marred by a proneness to error. Even the most honest of men, while giving themselves to the noblest of causes, make mistakes.

Perfection and absolute freedom from error are properly attributable only to deity. "The Rock, his work is perfect; for all his ways are justice: A God of faithfulness and without iniquity." (Deut. 32:4).

Since "to err is human," it would logically follow that the Bible is a mere human production if it does err on any point. But the absence of human error in a book which admittedly was written by fallible human beings would compel us to the conclusion that a supernatural guidance superintended those men so that the finished product of their labors was a divine production.

It is no little thing to hold that "minor mistakes" relating to "mere peripheral matters" are contained in Scripture. It is a serious charge and, if it could be proved, would destroy the Biblical doctrine of inspiration. No physician who was known to have made a number of fatal mistakes in diagnosing and treating minor ailments would be trusted in the most crucial of times when life was clearly in the balance. No book which errs in matters of history, geography or science could be trusted to tell us the perfect will of God.

Although numerous extensive lists of the alleged errors of the Bible have been produced by its critics, not one of these alleged inaccuracies has ever been finally settled to the discredit of Scripture. As Loraine Boettner has written:

> It gives us no little satisfaction . . . to know that as scholarship and archaeological discovery have advanced the great majority of the supposed "Biblical errors" which were so confidently paraded by skeptics and atheists a few decades ago have been

cleared up. Today scarcely a shred of the old list remains. It gives us even greater satisfaction to know that despite all of the merciless attacks which through the ages have been made on the Bible, and despite all of the fierce light of criticism which so long has been beating upon its open pages, *not so much as one single error has been definitely proved to exist anywhere in the Bible.* Without exception up to the present time where the conflict has been joined and the verdict rendered the skeptic has been proved wrong and the Bible right. Those supposed discrepancies remain today as only too readily forgotten warnings against those who in their eagerness to do violence to the scripture doctrine of inerrancy throw historical and literary caution to the wind.[2]

THE APPROACH TO PROBLEMS IN SCRIPTURE

The attitude one takes toward the criticism of the Bible is largely determined by his initial presupposition concerning the nature of Scripture. It is not that a so-called "conservative" student is any less scholarly and/or honest in his approach to the Bible than is his "liberal" counterpart. It is simply that the former, in view of the fact that the Bible has been repeatedly vindicated in the past, undertakes the historical-critical study of the Bible in the light of his faith in One who has assured us of its utter infallibility and confidently expects a thorough study of the problem at hand to do away with any apparent inaccuracy or self-contradiction whereas the latter, having abandoned the authority of the Lord, has no hesitation in announcing that the presence of an apparent error is indeed a case of "established error" in the Biblical record. Surely the latter approach is one which wrests the Scripture unto one's spiritual destruction. (Cf. 2 Pet. 3:16). Where a reasonable solution of a Biblical difficulty can be offered, there is no justification for adopting a dogmatic attitude and maintaining the presence of error.

Clark H. Pinnock has made the point:

Admittedly, evangelical criticism is conservative in a way negative criticism is not. Complete critical freedom is purchased at the price of Christian faith. This is a freedom we do not covet. We are reluctant to consider our inability to solve a given problem as proof that the problem is ultimately real (i.e., an error). Negative critics who do charge errors in Scripture usurp, we believe, the very infallibility for themselves which they deny to Scripture.[3]

Just one example of this difference in approach will suffice for the present. Negative critics of the Bible long held that Scripture erred in referring to a non-existent race of people called the Hittites. They affirmed that since their existence was unconfirmed from some external source, we were logically forced to the conclusion that they never existed at all. Was this a fair assumption? On the other hand, believers had to admit the lack of external confirmation for the Hittite nation but insisted that the final verdict was not in as yet. They said that further study and investigation would likely turn up concrete evidence for the factuality of the Bible. After all, they reminded the critics, had the Bible not been vindicated countless times in similar situations before?

In 1906 excavations were begun in central Turkey which uncovered the capital city of the Hittite empire! There had never been an error in the Bible on this point; it was only that archaeologists had not yet found its full external confirmation.

CHALLENGING THOSE WHO CHALLENGE SCRIPTURE

Quite often it is the case that those who charge the Bible with errors and self-contradictions cannot produce even one example in support of their charge. I was once engaged in conversation with a man who stated that he did not believe the Bible. "Why don't you believe it?" I asked. "Because it is just filled with all sorts of errors," he replied. I proceeded to hand him my Bible and said, "Show me just one." The man left in anger and apparently thought I had been unkind to him. But it is only fair to challenge those who challenge the Bible to give their evidence. In almost every case the person who is speaking so disparagingly of the Bible will be seen to be making a charge for which he has not the slightest bit of evidence. He has heard someone else *say* that Scripture is filled with errors and accepted that charge without honestly investigating the matter for himself.

The Bible does contain some very difficult matters. Some of these difficulties may at first appear totally incapable of solution to one encountering them for the first time. But it is a type of intellectual arrogance for one to decide that if a solution to the problem does not occur to him immediately there simply is no solution to be found! Perhaps someone else has studied the matter carefully and found a perfectly complete and final solution. Therefore, if you encounter such a problem, do not concede the matter without having done all the investigating and study possible.

When close study is given to the problem and when more complete knowledge of the subject is gained, the difficulty or apparent contradiction will vanish.

Practically all of the alleged errors in Scripture stem from six sources. In this chapter we shall give brief attention to each of these and illustrate them with Biblical texts. The next two chapters will then study a more extended series of problem passages using the material of this chapter as a foundation.[4]

Human Ignorance

One of the sources of alleged errors in the Bible is human ignorance. The criticisms of the Word of God for its references to the Hittites was a criticism based on human ignorance. The Scripture was right all along and men were criticizing from their ignorance.

A whole series of criticisms stemming from human ignorance have to do with the narrative of Abraham's life and times. The Bible's negative critics long held that the sections of Genesis treating the life of this great patriarch reflected customs and cultural situations which did not prevail in the Near East until a millennium later than the period assigned him in the Bible (i.e., ca. 2000 B.C.). For example, we were told that camels were unknown in that region of the world at the time Abraham is supposed to have lived and yet the Bible says that he had such animals. (Cf. Gen. 12:16). Yet in more recent times archaeologists have discovered carvings and even skeletons of camels in that region which date back at least as early as 3000 B.C. Abraham's home city of Ur has been excavated and is known to have been a great city. The more things we learn of ancient cities and customs of life, the more confidence we have that the Bible reflects a fully historical and reliable knowledge of those things. The loud criticisms of Genesis and its references to Abraham have lost their punch! The critics were arguing from ignorance!

FAILURE TO BE FAIR WITH THE BIBLE

Some of the alleged errors are due to a failure to read exactly what the Bible says. For example, some people think they have found a contradiction in the Genesis account of the origin of the human family. They allege that the Bible says that all men sprang from one source, that all people descended from Adam and Eve. They then say that Cain, the son of Adam and Eve, is said to have gone to the land of Nod and found a woman there to become his wife. "If everyone descended from Adam and Eve," the critics ask, "where did this woman whom Cain married come from?" If students had only been fair with the Bible, they would never have come up with such a criticism of it.

The Bible does not say that Cain went into the land of Nod alone and then found a woman already living there. It says that Cain "dwelt in the land of Nod" and that while living there he "knew his wife; and she conceived and bare Enoch." (Gen. 4:16-17). We logically conclude that he had a wife before he went to Nod, that she was one of the daughters of Adam and Eve mentioned in Genesis 5:4 and that Cain and his wife chose Nod as the place where they would live. The critics tried to make the story contradict itself; but, as it is recorded in the Bible itself, there is no contradiction or logical impossibility in it.

Often it is charged that the Bible contradicts itself as to the number of animals that Noah took into the ark. Critics point out that in one place the Bible says that two of every kind of animal were put into the ark and that in another place it says that seven of every kind were put on board. Here is another case where a close reading of the Bible itself will clear away the supposed error. One has only to read Genesis 7:2 closely and the matter is resolved: "Of every clean beast thou shalt take to thee seven and seven, the male and his female; and of the beasts that are not clean two, the male and his female." Another supposed error vanishes into thin air!

Misinterpretation of the Bible

Another source of Bible discrepancies is faulty interpretation by Bible readers. A whole host of people have commented on the fact that Paul and James "contradict" each other in their teaching about faith and works. It is argued that Paul teaches salvation by faith apart from works of obedience and that James contradicts Paul by saying that salvation is by works. The notion that these two writers contradict each other arises only from a lack of careful study into what they actually wrote. A close examination of the facts shows that both men teach that one is saved by faith when that faith leads him to perform the words of obedience which God has assigned in the Scripture. James wrote: "Ye see that by works a man is justified, and not only by faith." (James 2:24). Paul wrote: "For in Christ Jesus neither circumcision availeth anything, nor uncircumcision; but faith working through love." (Gal. 5:6). Where is the contradiction in these two positions? There is none.

Critics frequently point to the fact that Galileo was condemned as a heretic by the Roman Catholic Church because he taught that the sun was the center of our planetary system instead of the earth. But that terrible blunder by the Catholic hierarchy was not in any way due to the Bible's teaching. Scripture nowhere says that the earth is the center of the universe. That was a false position which the Roman Catholic Church advocated which brought her into conflict with the great scientist, Galileo. The Bible has never been in conflict with the established facts of science on any matter. It is only the false interpretations of the Bible which some people impose on it that conflict with science. The Bible and science agree that the earth is round, not flat. (Cf. Isa. 40:22; Prov. 8:27). The Bible and science agree that the earth is poised in space without any visible supports, not resting on the back of Atlas or on marble pillars. (Cf. Job 26:7). It is not the Bible that comes into conflict with science. It is false interpretation of the Bible.

No Single Author Claims to Tell Whole Story

Other critics of the Bible have pointed to the fact that the authors of the four Gospels contradict each other in their accounts of the words written on the superscription on Jesus' cross. Matthew says, "This is Jesus the King of the Jews." (Matt. 27:37). Mark says, "The King of the Jews." (Mark 15:26). Luke says, "This is the King of the Jews." (Luke 23:38). And John says, "Jesus of Nazareth, the King of the Jews." (John 19:19-20). Now where is the contradiction? These accounts are not contradictory. They are supplementary. It is altogether likely that the whole superscription was: "This is Jesus of Nazareth, the King of the Jews." No one of the Gospel writers gave the whole of what was written, but each gave the essential part, i.e., it was "The King of the Jews" who was put to death. Or it may be simply that the slight differences of wording reflect the fact that, as John tells us, the superscription was written not once but three times—"written in Hebrew, and in Latin, and in Greek."

The same kind of observation could be made about the accounts of the resurrection given by the Gospel writers. Each writer tells something that the other writers do not tell us, but no writer contradicts the others in any detail. Thus, in order to get the whole story, we must read all the accounts of the resurrection and put all the facts together.

Change in Circumstances

Men sometimes take random statements from the Bible and set them in opposition to each other in an effort to prove that the Bible is self-contradictory. They fail to take the historical setting of the statements into account. For example, "And God saw everything that he had made, and, behold, it was very good." "And it repented Jehovah that he had made man on the earth, and it grieved him at his heart." When these two statements are placed side by side there appears to be a contradiction. But if one takes the time to examine them closely, he sees there is no contradiction at all. The former statement, recorded in Genesis 1:31, was made concerning the created world before the entrance of sin. The latter, recorded in Genesis 6:6, was made over a thousand years later when man had reached such a state of degeneracy "that every imagination of the thoughts of his heart was only evil continually." (Gen. 6:5). Each of the statements was perfectly correct at the time it was spoken.

We might well compare this supposed contradiction in the Scripture to the following situation. A mother dressed her little girl in a clean, carefully ironed dress and sent her off to school with the loving observation, "You look prettier than you ever have before!" At the close of school the little girl, who accidentally spilled a tray of finger paints on her dress that day, walked into her house and heard her mother exclaim, "What a mess! You look awful!" Now the mother may have been perfectly correct in each of her statements; but there had been a great change in circumstances from the time of the first until the time of the second.

BLIND PREJUDICE OF THE CRITICS

Finally, let it be pointed out that many people simply do not want to be convinced that the Bible is the Word of God. Therefore, regardless of how much proof we produce in support of our faith, they will not be convinced. On the other hand, let any critic make a false and unsubstantiated charge against the Bible's accuracy and these same people will rise up to acclaim him a scholar of the first rank and will put complete confidence in the false charge he makes! To put it very simply, blind and dogmatic prejudice against the Bible is the motivating force behind much of the criticism directed toward it.

Men would not dare to treat any other book with the obvious prejudice which they exhibit in their approach to the Bible. Fair-minded men would cry out in horror at such a sight. Yet the Bible can be mishandled and unfairly criticized and only a relative few will show any sign of dismay.

The Christian does not ask the unbeliever or skeptic to blindly grant his contention that the Bible is the Word of God. He simply asks him to be fair with the evidence which is presented about the Bible. And if men will be open-minded and fair with such evidence, they will inevitably be led to the conclusion that the Bible is everything it claims to be!

Conclusion

Do not be alarmed, therefore, when men assail the Bible. The Bible will stand the test of investigation. In the face of criticisms and charges of error and self-contradiction in the Bible, the Christian stands firm in the confidence that honest investigation will show that the Bible is right and the critic is in error!

CHAPTER IX

Alleged Errors in the Old Testament

In this chapter and the one to follow, a number of alleged errors in Scripture will be examined in order to determine whether or not the Bible's claim to inerrancy can stand.

In order to confine the discussion and focus the problem, the material in these two chapters will deal with the phenomena of Scripture set forth by Dewey M. Beegle in his book, *Scripture, Tradition, and Infallibility*,[1] wherein he attempts to make a distinction between inspiration and inerrancy and to show that the former can be held without the latter.

> In the last analysis, a rejection of the doctrine of inerrancy involves primarily a mental readjustment. Nothing basic is lost. In fact, when all the evidence is examined, those essential elements which the advocates of inerrancy have cherished and sought to protect are more firmly supported than ever before.[2]

In contrast to his contention, this book has already demonstrated (in Chapter Two) that the Bible view of inspiration demands inerrancy. The notion of an inspired Bible which contains one or many errors—whether theological, historical, or scientific—is an impossibility from the point of view advanced by Jesus and his prophets and apostles.

Upon concluding his enumeration of a number of alleged errors in the Scripture, Beegle says:

> Truth is like a two-way street or a double-edged sword. Although facts confirm the biblical record in many instances, they also disprove it in other cases. In the last analysis we must let the truth cut both ways. The true biblical view of inspiration must account for all the evidence of Scripture. The peril of the view of inerrancy is its rigidity and all-or-nothing character. If only one of the illustrations discussed in this chapter is correct, the doctrine is invalidated.[3]

His reasoning is correct, but his conclusion that "the evidence of Scripture" does invalidate the doctrine of inerrancy is false. Just one established error in Scripture would invalidate the claim for Biblical inerrancy. Yet it is emphatically denied that Beegle has produced such invalidating evidence in his book. He has raised some difficult problems, but our study will show that he has not raised a single insurmountable obstacle to faith in the inerrancy of the Bible. This claim will be established in this chapter and the one following as each of Beegle's alleged errors is examined in turn.

In view of the fact that so many challenges have been hurled at the doctrine of inerrancy, one may question the purpose of examining the particular challenge of Beegle in such detail. The special significance of his challenge lies in the fact that he claims to stand in the "evangelical tradition" while giving it. Holding to the substantial authenticity, but not total inerrancy, of Scripture, he would establish another view of the Bible over against the two positions of absolute confidence or total rejection which have been traditionally held. His book has been an influential work among numerous conservative students of the Bible and has added a great problem to the task of maintaining a fundamentally Biblical view of propositional revelation.

QUESTIONS RELATIVE TO OLD TESTAMENT CHRONOLOGY

This chapter will set forth reasonable explanations of some chronological problems involved in the Old Testament. Definitive solutions to these problems will not be claimed, for part of the problem lies in the simple fact of scarcity of historical data. But adequate evidence will be shown to demonstrate that Beegle has not produced any established errors in the Old Testament.

It is freely admitted that some of the most perplexing problems in the study of the Bible have to do with matters of chronology. These problems are not solved by saying that the ancients simply were not as concerned about the accurate dating of events as we are today or that the Bible is not intended to be a textbook of ancient history.

The Bible contains great sections of historical data which relate directly to certain national events in Israel, to wars fought with certain Pharaohs of Egypt, or to the prescribed years of a certain king's reign. If the Bible is the literal Word of God to man, it must be absolutely reliable whenever it relates any of these matters. Errors with regard to the chronology set forth in the Bible would constitute no less serious a blow to the view of Biblical infallibility than errors with regard to specific events in the life of Christ or doctrines taught by the apostles and prophets of the early church. All of these matters are declared to have been recorded under the guidance of the Holy Spirit, but if any one of them proves unreliable then all the others must necessarily be held suspect. Thus, although some would dismiss matters of Old Testament chronology as unimportant, the student of the Biblical doctrine of inspiration must consider them as equally significant as any other information alleged to have been recorded accurately in the Scripture. A basic question is: Is the claim for accuracy in these matters true? If not, there is no reason why men should have confidence in the other matters related in the Bible and regard them as reliable accounts.

While it must be granted that no final disposition can be made of some of the problems of chronology with which we must deal in the Old Testament, enough information does exist for us to posit reasonable solutions to them.

And in the light of past experience with such problems (e.g., challenges to the historicity of the patriarchs), there is no reason to doubt that yet unanticipated finds will provide final and definite solutions for these.

Allen Bowman has suggested at least four factors which help to account for some of the chronological problems we confront in Bible study:

(1) Bible writers were not vitally interested in a strict chronological arrangement of their materials. . . . Many difficulties in harmonizing the four Gospels, for instance, spring from this source.
(2) The writers often used round numbers instead of more precise figures in referring to total days, weeks, or years.
(3) The Hebrews used two calendars, one for the sacred year and one for the civil year. The sacred year began with the month of Abib (the time of the exodus) at the autumnal equinox. . . . The civil year began with the vernal equinox, thus making the month Abib the seventh in the year. . . .
(4) In reckoning periods of time, the Hebrews counted parts of years or of days as full years or full days.[4]

Another important point to remember in this regard is this:

If, as we know to be a fact, the people to whom the Old Testament was originally addressed cared little or nothing about exact dates, used round numbers in reckoning, and were accustomed to overlapping reigns of kings and to telescoping genealogies as an aid to memory, then it cannot be urged as an argument against the historicity of the documents containing such things that there is no mathematical astronomical chronology in the Bible. Whatever the system of chronology was, the people to whom it was written understood it perfectly, and our ignorance of its exact nature cannot be used against the historicity of the Bible documents.[5]

In the course of his overall assault on the doctrine of Biblical inerrancy, Beegle includes three charges of error with regard to Old Testament chronology. In defending the basic affirmation of this book, it will be maintained that since plausible explanations can be given for these phenomena no one can positively claim to have shown them to be errors. Thus, as Edward Young has well said, "Where there is the possibility of a reasonable solution of a difficulty there is no warrant for adopting a dogmatic attitude and for maintaining the presence of error."[6]

THE REIGN OF PEKAH

The first difficulty advanced by Beegle involves the reign of Pekah in Israel. The Biblical statement concerning his reign is this: "In the two and fiftieth year of Azariah king of Judah Pekah the son of Remaliah began to reign over Israel in Samaria, and reigned twenty years." (2 Kings 15:27). With regard to the number of years assigned to Pekah as Israel's ruler, Beegle flatly states: "For some years now, the figure 20 has been known to be wrong."[7]

It is certainly to be admitted that the problems of chronology involved here are complex. As outlined by Beegle, the problem arises from a consideration of the following factors:

> The verse in question (15:27), says Pekah began to reign in the fifty-second year of Azariah (another name for Uzziah). Azariah's death, coming in the fifty-second year of his reign, occurred about 739 B.C., and therefore Pekah's reign began then. This was also the year in which Isaiah the prophet "saw the Lord . . . high and lifted up" (Isa. 6:1). If Pekah is given his twenty years, then he finished in 719. The Biblical record says Hoshea, the last king of Israel, followed Pekah and reigned for nine years. This would mean that Samaria, the capital of Israel, fell in 710. However, archaeological evidence has confirmed beyond doubt that Samaria submitted to the Assyrians in 722. It is impossible, then, to give Pekah his twenty years after 739 B.C.[8]

Beegle then proceeds to show how inadequately some have sought to deal with the problem. Some have simply counted backward from the fall of Samaria and postulated that Pekah's reign must have begun in 751 B.C. But this proposed solution will not work because it would put the chronology of Menahem, Israel's king twelve years before Pekah (763-753 B.C. by the restructured chronology of this proposed solution), into conflict with the accepted dates for his Assyrian contemporary, Tiglath-pileser III (745-727 B.C.).[9]

Others have accounted for the twenty years by suggesting that Pekah wanted to blot out the memory of the two kings who had ruled Israel before him for twelve years (Menahem and Pekahiah) and therefore altered Israel's court records so as to show himself to have ruled during their days of power. By this explanation the compiler of Second Kings simply copied the court records without discovering the error. But what would this do for the claim of supernatural guidance of the writers of Scripture so as to prevent them from including errors into their own accounts?

Finally, Beegle suggests, some have accounted for the "inaccuracy" here by saying that a scribal error in the transmission of 15:27 must be involved. But this cannot be the solution, for two synchronisms later in the book are based on the assumption of a twenty-year reign for Pekah.[10]

Beegle suggests that the compiler of Second Kings erred because he did not have the more absolute time scale which scholars of the period have now compiled in the light of Tiglath-pileser III and his dates. He further suggests that the actual reign of Pekah must have been only eight years.

His final jab is at those who contend for inerrancy of the autographs in spite of irreconcilable difficulties in our present copies. He writes: ". . . there is no other way but to admit that the erroneous details of 15:27, 32; 16:1 were in the original compilation of Second Kings."[11]

Beegle's treatment of this problem clearly reflects his presupposition concerning the nature of Scripture. One who accepts the Lord's assurances of the Bible's utter infallibility looks for a possible solution which will take all the known data into account, but Beegle has decided that this apparent error is in fact a real error which is incapable of being explained in any satisfactory manner.

If there is a reasonable solution to this difficulty, then Beegle is presumptuous in declaring it to be an established error. It is the contention of this writer that a plausible solution to this problem does exist.[12]

The suggestion has been put forth that the kingdom of Israel was divided for the first twelve years of the reign of Pekah. This would make the accession of Pekah contemporaneous with that of Menahem (752 or 751 B.C.)[13] and would provide an obvious and simple solution to the problem posed by Beegle. This would mean that Pekah's dates were 752-732 B.C., with part of his reign being over a divided kingdom.

But is there any evidence which would support such a suggestion, or is it simply postulated in order to attempt a defense of Biblical inerrancy? At least two lines of evidence seem not only to make this view possible but also probable as the solution to the problem.

First, there is the evidence from Assyrian records which refer to a situation which implies a division of the kingdom of Israel during the time of Menahem and Pekah.

> It is an interesting point—though the designation may be fortuitous—that in the Assyrian tablets Menahem is called 'Menahem of Samaria', whereas the reference to the overthrow of Pekah names his country as Bit Humria—the House of Omri, which is the normal Assyrian designation of Israel. It is possible that Menahem ruled only the district of Samaria, while Gilead and some of the northern section of the country were under the control of the official Pekah, who made himself independent. . . .
> This supposition means that Pekah established his independence during the reign of Asshurnarari V (754-745) who made no compaign into Syria. When Tiglath-pileser III appeared in the west, Menahem took the opportunity to enlist his support by sending tribute of a thousand talents of silver, with the idea—as 2 Kings xv 19 puts it—'that he might help him to confirm his hold of the royal power.' This expression may simply indicate Menahem's sense of insecurity in the presence of Assyrian power; but it may equally well indicate the presence of a rival.[14]

Against this view there is still the objection that it is

only an alternative theory based on the peculiarity of Assyrian records which is able to interpret 2 Kings 15:19 so as to fit itself. Is there any evidence from the Bible itself to the effect that such a divided situation existed in Israel at this time? Without this sort of evidence the case would appear to be rather weak.

Second, Biblical evidence for a situation of division in the northern kingdom is available in the book of Hosea. In chapters four and five of Hosea, there seems to be a clear distinction among three kingdoms—Israel, Ephraim and Judah. "For Israel hath behaved stubbornly, like a stubborn heifer . . . Ephraim is joined to idols; let him alone." (Hos. 4:16-17).

> I know Ephraim, and Israel is not hid from me; for now, O Ephraim, thou hast played the harlot, Israel is defiled. Their doings will not suffer them to turn unto their God; for the spirit of whoredom is within them, and they know not Jehovah. And the pride of Israel doth testify to his face: therefore Israel and Ephraim shall stumble in their iniquity; Judah also shall stumble with them. (Hos. 5:3-5).

Although most scholars assume that the names Israel and Ephraim are interchangeable as designations for the northern kingdom throughout its history,[15] Cook argues from a detailed analysis of Biblical data that "Ephraim was not used to denote the whole of the northern kingdom before the time when in fact the northern kingdom was reduced to the rump-state of Ephraim."[16] That this is not a unique position advanced simply in the hope of clarifying a difficult problem in Old Testament chronology for conservative students is evidenced in the fact that another scholar, writing on Ephraim without giving any direct reference to the problem under consideration in this study of chronology, has written:

> The basis for the use of "Ephraim" to designate Israel was provided by the unfortunate outcome of the Syro-Ephraimite War (734-732), in which the N [sic] kingdom of Israel saw itself robbed of its peripheral territories, which were turned into the Assyrian provinces of Dor, Megiddo, and Gilead; and Israel was reduced to its central territory, the old

settlement area of the tribes of Manasseh and Ephraim. Since Ephraim had long since overshadowed Manasseh in its importance, the designation of the rump state as Ephraim suggested itself automatically and endured, too, when this remnant was made into the Assyrian province of Samaria ten years later.[17]

Thus the way is clear to offer a positive solution to the difficulty of Pekah's reign. In the words of Cook:

> There remains now no obstacle to our taking seriously the biblical synchronizations for the reign of Pekah. He siezed [sic] control of parts of Israel east of the Jordan and in Galilee in 752 B.C. at the time when Menahem seized the throne in Samaria. Jotham of Judah began to reign (in the father Azariah's lifetime) in Pekah's second year, and after his sixteen years' reign, Ahaz succeeded him in Pekah's seventeenth year. Meanwhile the activity of the Assyrians in the west must have confined Pekah to Transjordania, while Menahem paid tribute to gain their support. Pekahiah succeeded Menahem; but after two years Pekah advanced with his Gileadites, killed Pekahiah, and became king in Samaria in 740 B.C. This date is synchronized with the Judaean dynasty as the 52nd year of Azariah (2 Kings xv 27). The divided northern kingdom thus lasted from 752 to 740. For the remaining eight years of his reign Pekah ruled Israel, from which Galilee was completely removed by 733. Pekah was deposed in 732 B.C.[18]

As Beegle suggested at the beginning of his discussion of this problem, he has followed the chronology set forth by Thiele in his standard work on the subject.[19] In Thiele's work, almost all of the problematical issues which had existed with regard to Jewish chronology were satisfactorily resolved except this one involving Pekah. Adding to Thiele this reasonable solution of the problem concerning Pekah, we may now say that the chronology of the Hebrew kings cannot be legitimately used against the Bible's absolute historical trustworthiness. In fact, it may be urged, as W. A. Irwin remarked in his introduction to Thiele's book, that it is a matter of first-rate importance to learn that the books of Kings are reliable in precisely those features that formerly stimulated only derision.[20]

THE REIGN OF HEZEKIAH

The second difficulty set forth by Beegle involves a problem of chronology in Judah with regard to Hezekiah. He writes:

> Another difficult chronological problem has to do with the dates of Hezekiah's reign. 2 Kings 18:1 states, "In the third year of Hoshea son of Elah, king of Israel, Hezekiah the son of Ahaz, king of Judah, began to reign." Hoshea began reigning in 731, when he slew Pekah (15:30). According to 18:1, then, Hezekiah began to reign about 728. But 18:13 notes that Sennacherib invaded Judah in "the fourteenth year of King Hezekiah." Since Sennacherib's campaign against Judah and Jerusalem was in 701, Hezekiah began his reign in 715. He ruled for twenty-nine years (18:2), that is, down to 686. This conclusion is also in line with the inference from 20:6 that after Hezekiah's illness (which occurred about the time of Sennacherib's campaign) God spared his life fifteen years. Practically all scholars are agreed now that Hezekiah reigned 715-686. Then what is to be done with 18:1, which seems to begin Hezekiah's reign in 728?[21]

The problem is thus clearly seen. Second Kings 18:1 seems to begin Hezekiah's reign in 728 B.C. while 18:13 would appear to date it from 715. Is there any way to bring about harmony in these two apparently contradictory statements?

Several attempts have been made to resolve this difficulty.[22] Although one or more of these attempts may be adequate to show that one ought to be very cautious about insisting upon the presence of error in Second Kings, it appears that the most reasonable and easily accepted of them is the one advanced by Kitchen and Mitchell.[23] All the apparent chronological mysteries can be dispelled if, as we know was the case with several kings prior to Hezekiah, we assume periods of co-regency in the southern kingdom. There would certainly be nothing unique about such a situation, for even in the case of David and Solomon we have such a circumstance in evidence. Kitchen and Mitchell postulate the co-regency of Hezekiah with Ahaz from 729 to 715 B.C. and with Manasseh from 695 to 686 B.C. The chronology of the divided monarcy, following this scheme, would then be as follows during the period under consideration:

Israel	Judah
	Jotham
	739-731
	(Co-regent from 750)
Pekah	
740-732	
(Counted his years from 752)	
Hoshea	Ahaz
732-722	731-715
	(Co-regent from 743; senior partner from 735)
Fall of Samaria	
722	
	Hezekiah
	715-686
	(Co-regent from 729)
	Manasseh
	686-641
	(Co-regent from 695)

In the first edition of his book, Beegle considers the possibility of this view of the problem and asks:

> Did Ahaz and Hezekiah, like Jotham, have twelve-year coregencies (making the synchronisms technically accurate) or was Pekah given twelve years beyond his actual reign (thus resulting in erroneous synchronisms)?[24]

He responds to his query with the admission that "It is difficult to prove which view is correct . . ."[25] In this statement there is the concession of the point made earlier in this chapter to the effect that no one can positively claim to have shown that there are errors in the Bible. Beegle grants that if the chronology just suggested is taken as the correct one, the account in Second Kings can be judged "technically accurate." He further grants that it is "difficult" to prove that we should not accept this as the solution to the problem.

In his newer edition of this material, Beegle has been less inclined to make such an open concession. He writes: "This solution is theoretically possible, but the probability is exceedingly remote."[26] As has already been argued and proved in this book, a "theoretically possible" solution is all the believer is obligated to set forth in order to disprove the charge of "error" in the Bible. But is this approach so "exceedingly remote" as to be incredible? Beegle's affirmation to this effect is couched in these words:

> What Kitchen and Mitchell are really saying, whether they realize it or not, is that somehow Uzziah (who died at 68), Jotham (who died at 45), and Ahaz (who died at 36) happened to appoint their sons as coregents exactly twelve years before each of their deaths. This takes some credulity.[27]

One might as reasonably dismiss the Old Testament account of the successive reigns of Saul, David, and Solomon on the basis of the fact that it asserts forty-year reigns for each. The united kingdom of Israel only had three kings. Are we guilty of "credulity" or some sort of intellectual dishonesty if we believe (even if the "probability is exceedingly remote") that these kings reigned for equal periods of time? Again, what is the likelihood that the eventful life of such a character as Moses would divide itself into three periods of forty years each? Or what of the fact that the figure "forty" occurs in so many settings (e.g., forty days and forty nights of rain at the time of the flood, forty days and forty nights of fasting by Jesus in the wilderness, etc.) in Scripture? Shall we hold all these accounts suspect because the "probability is exceedingly remote" that the number could be so extensively used in relation to events which are altogether dissimilar?

Beegle's "logic" is altogether faulty at this point. He betrays his presupposition of inaccuracies in the Bible rather than proving their existence by this sort of argument. He concludes:

> The plain fact is that the so-called twelve-year coregencies resulted from a scribe or some scribes in Judah trying to make sense of Pekah's twenty years when he reigned only eight in Israel. Accordingly, the synchronisms in 2 Kings 17 and 18 are just as erroneous as the information in 2 Kings 15:27 and 16:1.[28]

But this is begging the question, for 2 Kings 15:27 and 16:1 pertain to Pekah and the synchronization of his reign with the total chronology of both kingdoms. It has already been shown that Pekah's reign can be fitted into the picture without compromising the integrity of the record. Thus Beegle's final charge against Second Kings is to resort to begging the question.

The chronology of the divided monarchy given earlier (following Kitchen and Mitchell) is fully adequate to show that the reigns of Pekah in Israel and Hezekiah in Judah can be fitted in so as to do injustice to neither the Biblical record nor modern scholarship. Thus it is affirmed that no error has been shown in these two matters of chronology.

GENESIS 5

The third problem set forth by Beegle with regard to Old Testament chronology is weaker than the others he has advanced. It has to do with the old and oft-answered charge that the Bible dates the creation at 4004 B.C.

> The year 1973, being the year 5733 in Jewish tradition, puts the creation in 3760 B.C. On the other hand, many Christians have accepted the date 4004 B.C., determined by Archbishop James Ussher (1581-1656).
>
> It was not until the nineteenth century that enough evidence was available to disprove the 4004 date as the beginning of the world, and even today some Bibles still carry the old chronology.[29]

Here is a classic case of where ignorance of the Bible creates an apparent conflict between it and science. There are countless individuals who honestly believe that the creation of the world took place in 4004 B.C. and who would point to Ussher's chronology, printed in the margins of their King James Version Bibles, as proof of it. Yet the evidence available to scientists points to a very old earth, possibly several billion years old. The Bible simply says: "In the beginning God created the heavens and the earth."[30] The "beginning" could have been millions or billions of years ago. Or it could have been only a few thousand years ago—with the earth having been "aged" at the time God brought it into existence.

We just do not know when the creation of this planet occurred. The Bible does not tell us and scientific theories differ greatly. Is there a conflict between the Bible and science on this point? Has the Bible been shown to have been in error as to the age of the earth? Not at all. The conflict is between a *theory* advanced by a seventeenth-century theologian and certain *theories* advanced by modern-day scientists.

The genealogy given in Genesis 5 deals with "the generations of Adam"[31] down to the time of Noah. It does not provide an answer to the dating of the earth's age. It deals only with man and the length of time he has been on the created earth. To say the least, it definitely does not date the creation at 4004 B.C. or explain its nature in detail.

This genealogy, as opposed to many others given in the Old and New Testaments, does seem to claim completeness for itself. It gives the age of a man at the time of the birth of his son, the number of years he lived after the birth of that son and his age at the time of his death. If other recorded genealogies in the Bible picked up at Noah and gave as detailed information as this one gives, the procedure of Ussher for dating the creation of Adam would be valid. But in the absence of such it is mere presumption to attempt such a precise dating or to make positive claims for or against such an effort.

A demonstration of the unreliability of such a method is shown in this comparison:

Old Testament record | New Testament genealogy[32]
Joram (2 Kings 8:24) | Joram begat...
Ahaziah (2 Kings 8:25)
Joash (2 Kings 11:2)
Amaziah (2 Kings 14:1)
Uzziah (2 Chron. 26:1) | Uzziah

This comparison shows that, in accordance with typical Hebrew genealogies, the genealogies given in Scripture are not necessarily intended to provide us with exact chronologies. A genealogy is designed to show the line of family descent. In order to accomplish this purpose it is obviously unnecessary to show the exact lengths of time involved.

As Beegle pointed out, and has already been granted in this discussion of the matter, the author of Genesis 5 apparently intended to be chronological in his account of the generations of Adam. But this does not mean that we must accept 4004 B.C. as the date of creation. First, the other genealogies which would be necessary to establish an accurate dating are not given in the same fashion as this one. And, second, even if an end-to-end genealogy with specified times could be reconstructed, it would take us back only to the creation of Adam and not to the creation of the earth.

CONCLUSION

As Edward Young has said:

It is only candid to acknowledge that there are some problems of chronology for which no apparent solution is immediately forthcoming. At the same time one is on safe ground when he asserts that no man today is in the position of being able to prove that the Scriptures are guilty of error in their chronology, when that chronology is properly understood.[33]

Until such time as fully established solutions to some of these problems are forthcoming, as has been our experience with past criticisms leveled against the Bible's accuracy, we can set forth reasonable solutions which make it impossible for one to dogmatically assert the presence of established error.

CHAPTER X

Alleged Errors in the New Testament

Liberal critics of the Scriptures have frequently charged that Stephen's speech contains several serious historical errors. This, they allege, totally discounts the notion of inerrancy. The account in Acts presents Stephen as one who spoke under the control of the Holy Spirit. And worse still, when Luke recorded the speech, he did so in such a way as to indicate confidence in it. To say the least, he did not detect or feel the need to correct any part of it so as to remove alleged errors from it. This chapter will contend that Beegle is mistaken in alleging to have found errors in it.

PRELIMINARY CONSIDERATIONS

Stephen was an outstanding member of the Jerusalem church in its earliest days. He was judged by that church as a "man of good report, full of the Spirit and of wisdom" and thereby came to be appointed, under the personal supervision of the apostles, to a post of responsibility with regard to the daily ministration to needy widows. (Acts

6:3-6). Beyond his evident abilities as an administrator, Stephen was also a mighty evangelist. Preaching among unbelieving Jews of the city of Jerusalem, he encountered opposition of the strongest sort. With full confidence in the message he was preaching, Stephen entered into various synagogues and debated his opponents. Of the result of such debates, Luke writes: "And they were not able to withstand the wisdom and the Spirit by which he spake." (Acts 6:10).

Unable to withstand Stephen's wisdom, his opponents seized him, brought him before the Jewish council in Jerusalem and charged him with blasphemy. (Acts 6:11-14). Given the opportunity to defend himself before the Sanhedrin, Stephen traced the history of Israel from the call of Abraham to the building of Solomon's temple.[1] From this historical resume, he showed that the Jews had consistently followed a policy of persecuting true prophets and rejecting God's true word. He ended his speech with the stinging accusation that the Jews of his own time were guilty of the same sin of hardening their hearts against the truth which their forefathers had committed. Specifically, he charged that in their rejection of Jesus as the Christ they had committed the greatest of all sins in Israel's entire history.

In his presentation of the phenomena of Scripture which compel him to deny inerrancy, Beegle does not overlook this speech given by Stephen and recorded by Luke. He writes:

> Some commentators readily acknowledge that Stephen was mistaken, but they claim inerrancy for the autograph of the Acts in that Luke accurately copied Stephen's words, mistakes and all. However, this easy answer ignores the clear Biblical statement that Stephen spoke under the influence of the Holy Spirit. The difficulty, as Bruce implies, may well have arisen with Luke when he condensed Stephen's sermon. But with respect to the doctrine of inerrant autographs it makes no essential difference whether the telescoping occurred in Stephen's original speech or in Luke's condensation.[2]

Beegle is altogether correct in his claim that the source of the error—whether Stephen or Luke—would be immaterial. If the Scripture does contain an error at this point, then the Biblical doctrine of inerrancy is overthrown.

Before examining the two errors which Beegle alleges to have found in this speech, it should be pointed out that there is a strong presumption against the presence of error in it. Stephen was speaking before an audience thoroughly familiar with the Old Testament. His critics sitting on the council would likely have stopped him on the spot if his statements had been misrepresentations of the facts in the case.

Addressing himself to this point, Edward Young has said:

> The very fact that the Jews who heard Stephen did not make any outcry against him on the basis of his recital of the events of Old Testament history is most significant. True enough, they did make an outcry; they 'were cut to the heart, and they gnashed on him with *their* teeth'. (Acts 7:54). Why, however, did they do this? Was it because he had made errors in his recital of the events of Old Testament history? Not at all. With that recital of events they had no quarrel whatever. What arroused them was something quite different. What aroused them was Stephen's accusation that they had been the betrayers and murderers of the Just One, even Jesus. It was not Stephen's recital of history, but his application of that history, which caused the Jews to turn upon him.[3]

The supposition that a number of historical errors were committed in rather rapid succession and then left on record when they could have been easily corrected strains the imagination. Men who are constantly in the thick of controversy, as were the early Christians, do not leave themselves liable to refutation on such points as are presently being questioned by critics!

ACTS 7:4

The first difficulty set forth from Stephen's speech involves the call of Abraham and is stated thus by Beegle:

> In verse 4, Stephen states: "Then he departed from the land of the Chaldeans, and lived in Haran. And after his father died, God removed him from there

into this land in which you are now living." According to Genesis 11:26, Terah was 70 at the birth of Abraham, and he died in Haran at the age of 205. (11:32). Abraham, therefore, was 135 at the death of his father. However, Abraham left for Canaan when he was 75 (12:4), sixty years before the death of his father. One what grounds, then, does Stephen declare that Abraham left for Canaan "after his father died"? Neither the Hebrew nor the Septuagint supports this claim.[4]

Beegle concludes his summary of this problem by saying:

> There is hardly any way out but to admit that Stephen, even while under the inspiration of the Holy Spirit, probably made a mistake in declaring that Abraham left Haran after Terah died.[5]

Various solutions to this problem have been proposed. It has been suggested that the correct age of Terah at the time of his death, as given in Genesis 11:32, should be 145 instead of 205. This suggestion is largely dependent on the fact that the Samaritan Pentateuch gives this alternate figure. F. F. Bruce has suggested that since Philo agrees with Stephen that Abraham did not leave Haran until after his father had died there might have been a Greek version of Genesis 11:32 which agreed with the Samaritan Pentateuch and which served as the basis for the statement of Stephen and Philo.[6] It is not likely, however, that the Samaritan Pentateuch should be regarded as the original reading and that we would be justified in emending the Hebrew text upon the basis of such a reading.

Others have suggested that the statement "Terah died in Haran" could mean only that he died insofar as Abraham was concerned. Since Abraham never saw his father again after their separation in Haran, Terah was "dead" to him. A variant of this approach would understand the comment of Stephen and Philo to mean that Terah turned to idolatry in Haran and thus died spiritually. Abraham was therefore justified in leaving him as "dead" although his physical years were not yet numbered.[7]

Still another possibility is that Stephen is only referring to the order in which the events involving Terah and

Abraham are recorded in Genesis and not to their correct chronological sequence. In the Genesis account, the death of Terah is stated in 11:32 whereas the departure of Abraham from Haran is not referred to until 12:4. If it is the case that Stephen merely has reference to the order in which these events are stated in Genesis, his words "after his father died"[8] would be equivalent to "after the account of the death of his father."

A more reasonable solution to the problem would involve challenging the presupposition upon which Beegle's figures are calculated. He takes the statement in Genesis 11:26 to mean that Abraham was born in Terah's seventieth year. Does the statement, "And Terah lived seventy years and begat Abram, Nahor, and Haran," mean that all three sons were born in that same year? Or could it simply mean that Terah was without sons until he was seventy, after which age three male children were born to him? If the latter is the case, there would be no reason to think that the sixty years in question might not have passed between the time of the birth of Terah's first son and Abraham. By this scheme, Terah would have been 130 at the time of Abraham's birth and Abraham could have left Canaan at age 75 only after his father had died. Such a reconstruction of events does no violence to the Scriptural records involved and, in fact, shows itself to be favorably supported by related considerations.

For example, J. W. McGarvey has pointed out:

> The statement of the text, Gen. xi. 26, is that "Terah lived seventy years, and begat Abraham, Nahor and Haran." Unless we assume that these three were triplets, we can not assert that Terah was just seventy when Abraham was born. But that they were not triplets, and that Nahor and Abraham were much younger than Haran, is evident from the fact that Nahor's wife was Haran's daughter, and that Haran's son Lot was not many years younger than Abraham, as appears from the later history of the two . . . Stephen then may be relied on when he says that God removed Abraham from Haran into Canaan after the death of Terah; and if so, then the age of Terah when Abraham was born was 205 − 75 = 130 years.[9]

Edward Young objects to this solution by saying:

> If Abraham had been born when his father was so old, he would not have been skeptical about a son being born when he himself was at the age of one hundred. With what incredulity Abraham asks the question, 'Shall a *child* be born unto him that is a hundred years old?' (Gen. 17:17). Had his own father been one hundred and thirty years of age at Abraham's birth, it is not likely that the father of the faithful would later have exhibited such incredulity toward the promises of God.[10]

Replying to this objection against his proposed solution as offered by Alford, McGarvey pointed out:

> The learned author forgets that "in the course of nature" this same Abram, long after he was ninety-nine, and apparently after the death of Sarah, when he was one hundred and thirty-seven, took a younger wife and begat six other sons, the sons of Keturah. (Gen. xxiii. 1; xxiv. 1-4). The incredulity of Abraham, then, so far as it respected himself (for it is evident that it refers chiefly to Sarah), depended on something else than his mere age. It may have depended largely on the fact that he had now been living thirteen years with a young concubine, Hagar, since the birth of Ishmael, and she had not borne him another son. (xvii. 24, 25).[11]

Undoubtedly the reason for the difficulty we face in seeing the harmony between the speech of Stephen and the Old Testament account concerning Abraham lies in the fact that we do not know all the details of the patriarch's life. Taking the facts that we do have in the light of the speech of Stephen and the lack of criticism on this point by his enemies, it seems evident that the charge of error at this point is premature.

Acts 7:15-16

The second difficulty in Stephen's speech has to do with the sepulcher of Shechem and its purchaser. Beegle states the problem thus:

> In verses 15-16 we read, "And he [Jacob] died, himself and our fathers, and they were carried back to Shechem and laid in the tomb that Abraham had

bought for a sum of silver from the sons of Hamar in Shechem." Jacob was buried at Hebron (Mamre) in the field of Machpelah (Gen. 50:13), which Abraham had purchased from Ephron the Hittite (Gen. 23:16-18). Joseph, on the other hand, was buried at Shechem in the plot of ground which Jacob had purchased from the sons of Hamor (Josh. 24:32).[12]

It must certainly be admitted that the problems presented by this text are formidable. And even if it cannot be claimed that enough information is at hand to completely sweep away the difficulties connected with it, neither can it be claimed that there is no possible solution to them.

This text presents two points of apparent discrepancy: (1) it appears to say that Jacob was buried at Shechem whereas the Old Testament record clearly says he was buried at Hebron and (2) it attributes the purchase of the tomb at Shechem to Abraham whereas the Old Testament says that Jacob was the one who bought it. It would appear that Stephen had hopelessly confused the facts and that Luke has recorded those mistakes without bothering to correct them. Yet the point must be pressed again that if Stephen did actually commit such a gross jumbling of the facts it is strange that his audience (insofar as the record in Acts relates the event) did not challenge him. The members of the Sanhedrin knew the data concerning the lives of Abraham and Jacob and would not have been likely to let such matters as these go without challenge.

First comes the matter of the place of Jacob's burial. Beegle understands both "Jacob" and "our fathers" to be the common subjects of the verb "were carried." But is this necessarily the case? The English text could be understood to refer to the separate events of the death of Jacob and the eventual death of his sons, with the observation made concerning the sons only that they were eventually carried back to Shechem. Bruce so interprets the passage: "There Jacob died; there too, in due course, his sons died, but they were buried, not in Egypt, but in the land which God had promised to their children as their inheritance."[13]

The latter view of this passage has been taken by numerous older commentators and is given brief attention by Beegle. According to him, this view "splits the verse up and supplies words to make Stephen mean what Genesis and Joshua say."[14] He thereby implies that this is an arbitrary exegesis which is demanded only by a desire to retain the doctrine of inerrancy. This is not the case. There are linguistic considerations which support this view and show that this interpretation of the passage is altogether admissable.

J. W. McGarvey addresses himself to this matter by writing:

> The verb rendered died is in the singular number, ἐτελεύτησεν, and it agrees only with αὐτός, himself. The plural substantive "fathers" is not the subject of that verb, but of the plural ἐτελεύτησαν understood. The construction having been changed with the introduction of the plural subject, it follows that the plural verb μετετέθησαν, "were carried," belongs to fathers, and not to Jacob. The two clauses, properly punctuated, and with the ellipsis supplied, read thus: "and he died; and our fathers *died*, and were carried over into Shechem."[15]

The Old Testament informs us that Joseph's body was embalmed and eventually buried in Shechem after the exodus of the Jews from Egypt. (Gen. 50:26; Josh. 24:32). It is completely silent with regard to the brothers of Joseph. That their bodies should have also been transported into Canaan for burial is not at all unlikely. It is only from Stephen's statement that we have any actual confirmation of this event.

A complicating factor is added when Beegle points out: "According to Josephus (*Antiquities*, II, 8, 2), all the sons of Jacob, except Joseph, were buried at Hebron."[16] But this does not appear to be a great weight against the position just set forth. In the first place, since the Old Testament does not relate this information, Josephus' statement simply proves the existence of two traditions about the burial of the "fathers." The tradition with which Josephus was inclined to agree placed their bodies at Hebron, whereas the tradition accepted by Stephen and his audience of Sanhedrin members placed them at Shechem. Granted that two traditions did exist, who is to say that Josephus' judgment should be given more weight than that of Stephen and the members of the Jewish council at Jerusalem? Or, secondly, it might be argued that the bodies of the brothers of Joseph were temporarily interred at Hebron until the time of their removal at the exodus. The two traditions would then not be contradictory but complementary.[17]

The second difficulty in this text is that it attributes the purchase of the tomb at Shechem to Abraham whereas the Old Testament says that Jacob was the one who bought it.

Beegle himself acknowledges three possible solutions to this problem. First, it may be that something so simple as a scribal error brought about the substitution of the name "Abraham" for "Jacob." Beegle is quick to say: "This conjecture, however, is without any textual basis."[18] While granting his objection, it is not impossible that some very early copyist of the book of Acts either erred in his work or else took it upon himself to correct Stephen. Recalling the purchase made by Abraham and not remembering that Jacob made a similar one at Shechem, the copyist may have emended the text accordingly by inserting the name of the former patriarch.

There are others who "suggest the possibility that Jacob bought again at a later time a field previously purchased by Abraham."[19] Among more recent conservative commentators, Lenski indicates his favor for this view of the difficulty as over against scribal error.

> ... in Gen. 12:6 Abraham is in Shechem long before Jacob was there; and it is not at all improbable that Abraham made the original purchase, but after his departure from this place the land was again occupied by its original owners until Jacob repurchased it as Gen. 33:19 reports.[20]

Still another possibility mentioned by Beegle is the suggestion by F. F. Bruce that the two purchasers of land by the two eminent figures in Israel's history were "telescoped" in this text.[21]

Of these and other possible explanations for the appearance of Abraham's name in this text, it seems most likely that the suggestion of scribal error or emendation offers the most reasonable position and involves the fewest difficulties. After all, the claim of inerrancy applies only to the original manuscripts of the Biblical books and does not imply any sort of supernatural guidance for copyists who dealt with them at later dates.

To say the very least, these many possibilities of reasonable explanation take away one's right to label the difficulties considered in this chapter "errors."

The charge of errors in the speech of Stephen is improper. Again, although definitive solutions may not be available for certain difficulties in this speech, plausible explanations can be set forth to show that Scripture can be explained (without abandoning factual evidence or straining one's imagination to the extreme bounds) so as to avoid a discrepancy at the point of Beegle's charges.

GALATIANS 3:17

The next three phenomena set forth by Beegle appear designed to demonstrate that the writers of certain New Testament texts reflect discrepancies of understanding in their productions. If this point be established, its significance against the doctrine of Biblical inerrancy is immediately apparent.

Beegle alleges that Paul reflected a common incorrect tradition of his time when he supposedly allowed only 215 years for Israel's stay in Egypt.

In Galatians 3:16-17, Paul writes:

> Now to Abraham were the promises spoken, and to his seed. He saith not, And to seeds, as of many; but as of one, And to thy seed, which is Christ. Now this I say: A covenant confirmed beforehand by God, the law, which came four hundred and thirty years after, doth not disannul, so as to make the promise of none effect.

The difficulty involved in this text centers on the number of years mentioned by Paul. Beegle states the problem as follows:

> All the Greek manuscripts have 430, so in all liklihood Paul's original letter had it as well. There is

a problem with this figure, however. Abraham was 75 when he went to Canaan (Gen. 12:4), he was 100 when Isaac was born (21:5), Isaac was 60 when Jacob was born (25:26), and Jacob was 130 when he went to Egypt (47:9). Adding together 25, 60, and 130 gives 215 years in Canaan. The Hebrew text of Exodus 12:40 notes, "The time that the people of Israel dwelt in Egypt was four hundred and thirty years." Therefore, the time from the promise to Abraham to the giving of the law was 645 years (215 + 430). Did Paul get his information from another source, or did he mean something else when he wrote the number 430?[22]

Beegle suggests that Paul may well be following the reading of the Septuagint with regard to Exodus 12:40. Its rendering differs from the Hebrew text in that it says, "The time that the people of Israel dwelt in Egypt *and in the land of Canaan* was four hundred and thirty years." This would allot 215 years to Canaan and 215 years to Egypt and apparently solve the problem.

Yet this view is admittedly beset by too many difficulties to appear a likely solution in this case. For one thing, there is no ground for holding that the Septuagint should be preferred over the Hebrew text of Exodus. The Hebrew text is most likely the correct one and properly assigns 430 years to Israel in Egypt.[23] For another, it is unlikely that the rather small family of Jacob could have multiplied so as to number more than 600,000 males in the short period of 215 years. (Cf. Gen. 46:27; Ex. 12:37). Added to these considerations is the fact that the preponderance of archaeological evidence available on the subjects favors the 430-year stay in Egypt. It is therefore likely that Beegle is correct in rejecting the alternate reading of the Septuagint as the solution to this problem.

However, this does not give him the right to assert:

> Evidently it seemed good to the Holy Spirit to let Paul use the traditional 430 years without informing him that he was technically wrong and should be using 645 years as found in the Hebrew.[24]

There are other possibilities with regard to this problem which should be given consideration. Arndt has pointed out Paul's calculation of the 430-year period does not necessarily begin at the time when God first made his promise to Abraham. If this had been the beginning point of the calculation, 645 years should have been the figure. Instead, the initial terminus of the computation "may very well be the time when Jacob entered Egypt, on which occasion the Lord once more appeared to him and renewed His glorious promise as to the future greatness of Israel."[25]

Young follows Arndt in this matter and writes:

> Perhaps, if we examine the purposes of the Apostle, we may find a clue to the solution. Paul is making a contrast between the giving of the promise to Abraham and the giving of the law. It is when we consider the emphasis that the Apostle places upon these two termini that we realize that his intention is not to state precisely the length of the sojourn of the Israelites in Egypt. His purpose, therefore, differs from that of Stephen, from the passage in Exodus, and also from that in Genesis. It is well to keep in mind this consideration that Paul is not primarily concerned, as was Stephen, to state the length of the sojourn in Egypt. Before one asserts that there is a positive contradiction between the two, he must take into account the fact that the intentions and purposes of the two were not the same.[26]

Having set forth the differences in purpose between Paul's statement of this figure and other passages dealing with the same period, Young concludes:

> It is quite possible, then, in the light of his purpose, and his mentioning Abraham and his seed, that Paul simply wishes to set in contrast the whole period of the giving of the promise, namely, the so-called patriarchal period, with that of the giving of the law. Between these two there was approximately four hundred and thirty years . . . Thus, on this view, the two termini mark the period of the patriarchs, the period of the giving of the promise, and the period of the giving of the law. If this is the purpose of the Apostle, no fault can be found with his method. It is a perfectly possible construction, and if we have interpreted Paul correctly, there certainly is no conflict between what he says and the other passages with which he is alleged to stand in contradiction.[27]

Beegle grants that an interpretation such as that proposed by Arndt and Young would show that Paul was correct and in accord with the Hebrew text of Exodus 12:40. He denies that this is a correct interpretation, however, on the ground that Paul's argument in this passage "hinges not on periods of time but on events in Israel's history."[28] Specifically, he argues that the event of confirmation with regard to God's covenant with Abraham was that recorded in Genesis 15 and summarized in the eighteenth verse of that chapter: "In that day Jehovah made a covenant with Abraham..."

It would be a mistake, however, to contend that this was the only time the covenant was confirmed between God and Abraham. It was renewed and confirmed in the events of Isaac's birth and Abraham's willingness to present his son as a sacrifice before Jehovah. (Gen. 21-22; cf. 22:16-18). It would also be a mistake to overlook the fact that the covenant originally made with Abraham was repeated and confirmed with both Isaac (Gen. 26:4) and Jacob. (Gen. 28:14).

It is therefore not unreasonable to suppose that it was from the time of the confirmation of the Abrahamic covenant with his grandson, Jacob, that Paul was counting the interval which extends to the giving of the law of Sinai.

Beegle counters this by asking:

> What justification is there, then, for interpreting Paul to mean 430 years after the patriarchal period closed (that is, when Jacob went to Egypt)? Had he wanted to say this, would he not have expressed himself more explicitly?[29]

We are not in a position to explain why Paul did not express himself differently so as to remove any possibility of a difficulty in this text. We would as well wonder why any Biblical statement is so stated as to demand more than a casual reading for its complete understanding.

In order to prove that an actual error exists in this text, one would have to prove that Paul's intentions in using the 430-year figure were exactly the same as those of both Stephen and Moses when they used the same figure for their purpose. He would have to show beyond question that exactly the same period of time, bounded by the same events, was under consideration. Since this certainly cannot be done in this instance, the charge of an error's having been committed is not established.

On the other hand, the solution offered in this consideration of the problem is seen to be a reasonable one in light of the fact that Scripture repeatedly mentions Abraham, Isaac and Jacob together in connection with the covenant Paul was referring to in Galatians. In particular, when this covenant is the topic of discussion, the three patriarchs are grouped together and treated as if they were one.[30] This being true, who is to say that Paul did not use the name of Abraham, with whom the covenant originated, to include the other patriarchs who were also participants in its subsequent ratification?

MARK 14:30, 72

The next problem pointed to by Beegle is perhaps the weakest of all those phenomena which he raises in an effort to show the doctrine of inerrancy a false one. The problem centers on two verses in Mark as they relate to parallel accounts of the same event in Matthew and Luke.

Mark quotes Jesus on the eve of his crucifixion and represents him as saying to Peter, "Verily I say unto thee, that thou today, even this night, before the cock crow twice, shalt deny me thrice." (Mark 14:30). Then, in his reporting of the events which later transpired that night, Mark wrote:

> And straightway the second time the cock crew. And Peter called to mind the word, how that Jesus said unto him, Before the cock crow twice, thou shalt deny me thrice. And when he thought thereon, he wept. (Mark 14:72).

In his statement of the problem this account presents in relation to the other synoptic Gospels, Beegle writes:

> This same pattern (prediction by Jesus, occurrence of the event, and Peter's remembrance of the prediction) is also found in Matthew (26:34, 74-75) and Luke (22:34, 60-61). However, both of these accounts omit the words "twice," "second time," and "twice." In short, they report that Jesus said, "Be-

fore the cock crows, you will deny me three times."[31]

Beegle correctly points out that the difference in reading cannot be put down to scribal error for the manuscript evidence is too strong for the accepted text of Mark. He also dismisses the suggestion that Matthew and Luke "generalized the cock's crowing twice to mean 'shall not have finished crowing'."[32]

The fact that the parallel accounts of this series of events do not contain equal amounts of detail in no way denies the accuracy of any one or all of them. As Preus has pointed out:

> Inerrancy does not imply verbal or intentional agreement in parallel accounts of the same event . . . However, it must be clearly recognized that incomplete history or an incomplete presentation of doctrine in a given pericope is not false history or a false presentation.[33]

Matthew and Luke are evidently viewing the night in its entirety and referring to the cock-crowing which signalled the dawning of day. Mark is evidently viewing the night in its details and indicates that Peter's denials began around midnight, the time of the first cock-crowing, and ended prior to the dawning of the morning, the time of the second cock-crowing.

Geldenhuys has addressed himself to this point and said:

> In the New Testament the night, according to the Roman usage, is divided into four watches: 6-9 p.m., 9-12 p.m.; 12-3 a.m., 3-6 a.m. The third night watch the cock crows. It is indeed a fact that the cocks crow practically regularly at about 3 a.m. Occasionally, however, it does happen that they crow at about midnight. The regular time for the cock-crow is, however, about 3 a.m. When, therefore, as in Matthew xxvi, Luke and John xiii, cock-crow in general is mentioned, the time of the night is meant which ends about 3 a.m. Mark, however, states that Jesus said: "before the cock has crowed twice," and mentions in his account of Peter's denial that during that night a cock-crow was heard twice (one before and one just after Peter's third denial). We observe throughout how (as tradition also

teaches) in Mark there are numerous indications that it was especially Peter's personal recollections that were recorded in that Gospel. It is, moreover, obvious that, especially in such a case as the prediction concerning this denial and the denial itself, Peter would have had an ineffaceable recollection of the smallest details of the Saviour's words and the succeeding events. So we are not surprised that in Mark the prophecy and course of the events are described in greater detail than in the other Gospels.[34]

It can be confidently asserted that there is no contradiction involved in these accounts. Mark's account is not a case of discrepancy but of fuller information. Here, as in many other cases in the Gospels, the different accounts of the same episode are seen to be complementary. There is certainly no justifiable ground for alleging error at this point.

1 CORINTHIANS 3:19

The next difficulty posed by Beegle has to do with a quotation from the Old Testament given by Paul. He writes:

> Paul, in writing to the church at Corinth, said: "For the wisdom of this world is folly with God. For it is written, 'He catches the wise in their craftiness'." (3:19). The source of the quotation is Job 5:13, which is part of the first speech of Eliphaz the Temanite. Traditionally speaking, Eliphaz has never been considered as inspired ...
> Certain evangelicals more or less equate the expressions "It is written" and "God says." It cannot mean this in 1 Corinthians 3:19 if Eliphaz is uninspired. Apparently Paul did not care who said it, nor whether it was inspired.[35]

This criticism is unjustified. It will shortly be shown that the quotation of an uninspired individual or even an apocryphal book does not imply endorsement of the entire teaching of that individual or writing. In this particular case, the expression "It is written" would be the equivalent of "It is contained in Scripture." Thus Paul's statement could be used to argue for the canonicity of the book of Job but not for the inspiration for Eliphaz when he is quoted in that book.

Paul indicated that the words quoted from Eliphaz were true. In Job 5, Eliphaz made a wrong application of the truth he stated. Nevertheless the words themselves were true and they are contained in Scripture. This is all that Paul claimed.

Beegle comments:

> This illustration does not involve an error as such, but it does show how biblical evidence is often at variance with some of the more precise formulations of inspiration.[36]

This point is not valid. A precise formulation of the doctrine of inspiration takes into account the point just established, viz. that the quotation of an uninspired man does not imply endorsement of everything he said or any false application he may have made of certain truths. Thus this particular passage in no way mitigates against the case for Biblical inerrancy.

JUDE 14

In verse 14 of the brief epistle of Jude is found this statement: "And to these also Enoch, the seventh from Adam, prophesied, saying, Behold, the Lord came with ten thousands of his holy ones. . . ."

Most New Testament scholars hold that the quotations given by Jude at this point are from a pseudepigraphical book, the *Book of Enoch* 1:9 and 5:4. This book was known in the early Christian era and was defended as canonical by such men as Clement of Alexandria and Tertullian.

Beegle points to the fact that Jude cites this book and attributes the prophecy involved to "Enoch, the seventh from Adam." The point of Beegle's criticism is clear. Jude cites a recently written work which eventually was rejected from the New Testament canon and attributed it to a man who lived centuries before that time. Either Jude did not know the true source of the statement he quoted or else he incorrectly attributed the source to the Enoch of antiquity.

On the other hand, Jude quotes 1 Enoch 1:9 as a *prophecy* which is being fulfilled in his day. Would

> he have done so had he thought the book and the passage originated during the period between the Testaments? Does not the cruciality of the quotation indicate, rather, that Jude thought the authority of his source derived from Enoch, the preflood patriarch, who was taken up by God when he was 365 years old?[37]

And again:

> Jude did not intend to deceive or falsify the issue. His error was an innocent one which he made in common with his fellow Jews and Christians. But sincerity of motive did not eliminate the mistake. Moreover, the Holy Spirit did not override the human concept of Jude. How, then, does this accord with the dogma that the Holy Spirit "bore" the writers along, guiding them inerrantly in all that they wrote? The seriousness of the problem is also indicated by the fear of many even to recognize the difficulty; for example, commentaries by evangelicals seldom discuss the problem.[38]

Various solutions to this problem have been offered by those who hold to the high view of Scripture set forth earlier in this volume. Lenski, for example, denies that Jude quoted from the *Book of Enoch* at all.

> Why grant the writer of the *Book of Enoch* an ancient source and deny it to Jude? Consider the case of "Jannes and Jambres" (2 Tim. 3:8), where we cannot point to a source that was similar to the *Book of Enoch;* yet even if we could, that would not prove that Paul obtained the names from such a book, for again we ask: "Where did such a book obtain them?" So much for the source.[39]

But even if it be granted that Jude was quoting from an apocryphal book, does that mean that he erred in using such a source or in some way discredited his epistle by doing so? The quotation of an uninspired book does not imply endorsement of the book's entire content. Granting the possibility of Jude's use of a non-canonical book, Moorehead points out:

> Paul cites from three Greek poets: from Aratus (Acts 17:28), from Menander (1 Cor. 15:33), and from Epimenides (Tit. 1:12). Does anyone imagine that Paul indorses all that these poets wrote? To the quotation from Epimenides the apostle adds,

"This testimony is true" (Tit. 1:13), but no one imagines he means to say the whole poem is true. So Jude cites a passage from a non-canonical book, not because he accepts the whole book as true, but this particular prediction he receives as from God.[40]

The question of significance with regard to Jude's use of this prophecy is not the naming of the immediate source of the words but the reliability of the source. Whether oral tradition, the *Book of Enoch* or some other source provided the words of the prophecy to Jude, the crucial matter is whether or not he was correct in using the quotation.

There is nothing about the Biblical doctrine of inspiration which would preclude the use of an uninspired source document by a writer. The doctrine of inspiration would guarantee, however, that the writer would properly distinguish between true and false information in those reports and use the true information in only such ways as to impart truth accurately. Nothing Beegle advances counts against this view.

Jude 14 assures us that the Enoch of antiquity, "the seventh from Adam,"[41] did indeed make a certain statement. That statement was true. Regardless of the manner in which it was brought to Jude's attention, Jesus' view of Scripture holds that it was authenticated by the Holy Spirit when he caused Jude to cite it.

JUDE 9

Another reference in Jude to an event not otherwise related in the Bible is in verse 9. In contrast to certain false teachers who spoke with great arrogance, Jude wrote of the great restraint shown by Michael the archangel. "But Michael the archangel, when contending with the devil he disputed about the body of Moses, durst not bring against him a railing judgment, but said, The Lord rebuke thee."

The account of the burial of Moses' body is contained in Deuteronomy 34:6. No reference is made in the context to any contest over the body. That the story of some sort of contest was current among the Jews is clear from Rabbinic literature. It also appears certain that this story was related in the pseudepigraphical *Assumption of*

Moses.[42] That such could have been the case and that Jude could have possibly referred to that story is enough to cause Beegle to allege another blow to inerrancy.

> Either the archangel Michael contended with the devil for the body of Moses or he did not. Joshua and the prophets never refer to any such struggle, so there is no Biblical reason, aside from Jude's allusion, for believing in the actuality of the story. On the other hand, does not the authoritative function of Jude's illustration show the importance that he attached to it. If, as the evidence seems to indicate, Jude accepted the current tradition with respect to the body of Moses, what becomes of the doctrine of inerrancy?[43]

The same criticisms offered against Beegle with regard to Jude's alleged use of the *Book of Enoch* apply with telling force here. An uninspired document could reflect a tradition rooted in actual fact. An inspired writer could quote certain lines from that document and thereby endorse that tradition as correct without giving a blanket endorsement to everything contained in it. The point is again emphasized that the process of inspiration did not function to provide facts so much as to enable the writer to sift out the data and include only the true facts in his writings. The basic affirmation of this book requires only that a plausible explanation be offered which would allow for correctness in the Biblical account. This has been done.

Beegle is altogether unjustified in attacking the doctrine of inerrancy based on two possible references to noncanonical works in the book of Jude. Jude may be citing Jewish tradition which served as the basis of the apocryphal stories in both cases. There simply is not enough evidence to settle this point. But even if he is alluding to these uninspired documents, the allusion tells us nothing of his view of the pseudepigrapha generally. It tells only of his acceptance of the actuality of the prophecy and event to which he refers.

What becomes of the doctrine of inerrancy in the light of Jude and the possible relationship this epistle has to apocryphal works? It stands as our guarantee of discrimination between mere legend and actual fact when uninspired sources are used by Spirit-borne men.

CONCLUSION

The difficulties dealt with in these last several pages have been shown to have reasonable solutions which harmonize all the known data of Scripture, history and related considerations. It is therefore denied that any of the phenomena set forth by Beegle controvert the claims made by Jesus Christ for the total inerrancy of Scripture.

In his classic work in defense of the verbal inspiration of Scripture, Warfield wrote:

> No phenomena can be pled against verbal inspiration except errors,—no error can be proved to exist within the sacred pages; that is the argument in a nut-shell. . . . Modern criticism has absolutely no valid argument to bring against the church doctrine of verbal inspiration, drawn from the phenomena of Scripture.[44]

This same bold claim can still be made today.

CHAPTER XI

The Transmission and Translation of Scripture

The burden of this book up to this point has been to show that the Bible, as originally given through men in its various parts, was a gift from God and therefore true, complete and authoritative. Men were not left to give their own opinions or mere personal feelings about matters discussed in Scripture; they were fully borne along by the Holy Spirit so that every word they wrote was a God-breathed word. But even if this be granted about *Scripture as it was originally given* (i.e., the autographs), what confidence do we have that its contents have not been revised or altered in the long process of transmission and translation through which our English Bible has come into our hands? Can one know that he possesses the original message God gave to men through the apostles and prophets? It is to this problem that we turn our attention in this chapter.

THE PROVIDENCE OF GOD

When one first begins to contemplate this matter of transmission and translation, a rather obvious presupposition comes early to mind. *If the original manuscripts of the various Biblical books were brought to be as the result of the workings of Almighty God, surely the same God has seen to the providential preservation of their contents through the ages.* Heaven's work of communication with lost humanity so as to bring us to salvation would be an imperfect work if the process were not overseen and brought to successful fruition. But this would be a logical impossibility for God, for "his work is perfect" (Deut. 32:4) and his "faithfulness is unto all generations." (Psa. 119:90).

It is rather absurd to suppose that God would go to the great lengths he did for the original writing down of his truth and then abandon the process of revelation so that no assurance is possible for generations far removed from the autographs of Scripture!

The fact that we do have the text of the Bible as it was originally given does not rest upon presupposition alone. An important field of Biblical study is called *textual criticism* and concerns itself with meticulous investigations into the reliability of the text of the Bible. Let us turn to an examination of some of the data provided us by the textual critics.

Concerning the Old Testament

There are no original manuscripts of any Old Testament books available to the textual scholars. Yet from what they have learned about the painstaking copying and preservation of the books at the hands of Jewish professionals, there is every reason to have confidence in the Old Testament which has been preserved for us.

During the period from approximately 300 B.C. to A.D. 500, the duty of preserving and transmitting the Hebrew Bible fell to the ancient scribes or *Sopherim*. These men took extreme care to preserve the text in as pure a form as possible, including the counting of the letters in their manuscripts!

The work of the scribes ended around A.D. 500 and in their place arose the Massoretes.

The Massoretes were the custodians of the sacred traditional text, and were active from about A.D. 500 to 1000. They continued and completed the objectives of the *Sopherim* and the rabbis by definitely fixing a form of the Hebrew text, which subsequently became known as Massoretic. Accordingly they concerned themselves with the transmission of the consonantal text as they had received it, as well as with its pronunciation, on the basis that the text itself was inviolable and every consonant sacred.[1]

All this points to the fact that Scripture was given the highest possible regard and every possible precaution was taken to assure the purity of the sacred text. The copying of Old Testament manuscripts was no haphazard thing which is to be regarded with disdain by modern men. To the contrary, it was a far more meticulous thing than modern men are willing to undertake in their impatience and haste.

We are still left with the question, however, as to how well the process actually worked. Does the Massoretic Text faithfully represent the Hebrew Bible as orignally given and as known, for example, by Jesus and his apostles? A series of events dating from 1947 enables us to answer this question with explicitness.

Before 1947 the oldest manuscript of any Old Testament book known to us was from around A.D. 900. In that year a discovery was made in a cave near the northwestern edge of the Dead Sea which has been far-reaching in its consequences. The Qumran caves have yielded Biblical manuscripts from every book in the Old Testament except Esther and discoveries are still being made. These documents survive from a Jewish religious sect which had established a separate community in the Judean desert from about 150 B.C. to about A.D. 70. The people living in this little community spent much of their time studying and copying Scripture. When it became apparent to them that their land was going to be overrun by the Romans, they put their precious scrolls in earthenware jars and hid them in caves near the Dead Sea. Following the destruction of Jerusalem, the former inhabitants of the little community never returned and their library of manuscripts went undetected until 1947.

The great significance of the Dead Sea materials is their testimony to the accuracy of transmission of the Old Testament. The scrolls of Qumran were approximately one thousand years older than any of the manuscripts Old Testament scholars had been working with prior to their discovery. By a careful comparison of the Dead Sea Scrolls with the Massoretic Text, textual critics could now get a clear indication of the accuracy of transmission of the Old Testament over a period of a millennium! What was revealed by such a study?

> For example, we may study the copy b of Isaiah. The text is extremely close to our M.T. A comparison of Isaiah 53 shows that only seventeen letters differ from the M.T. Ten of these are mere differences of spelling, like our "honor" or "honour," and make no change at all in meaning. Four more are very minor differences, such as the presence of the conjunction which is often a matter of style. The other three letters are the Hebrew word for "light" which is added after "they shall see" in verse 11. Out of 166 words in this chapter only this one word is really in question and it does not at all change the sense of the passage.
>
> This is typical of the whole manuscript. Even the use of vowel letters and the preservation of archaic grammatical forms are exceedingly close to the M.T.[2]

Of the Dead Sea Scrolls and their testimony to the accuracy of transmission of the Old Testament, Gleason L. Archer has written:

> Even though the two copies of Isaiah discovered in Qumran Cave 1 near the Dead Sea in 1947 were a thousand years earlier than the oldest dated manuscript previously known (A.D. 980), they proved to be word for word identical with our standard Hebrew Bible in more than 95 per cent of the text. The 5 per cent of variation consisted chiefly of obvious slips of the pen and variations in spelling.[3]

In addition to the valuable manuscripts of various Old Testament books, there are also some other important sources which the textual critic can use in determining the original text of the Hebrew Bible. These sources consist of various versions (i.e., translations) of the Old Testament.

The most important of these versions is the Septuagint, a translation of the entire Old Testament into the Greek language. This version was begun around 250 B.C. and was the Bible of the earliest Christians. Luke especially reflects the Septuagint in his writings. A rather free translation of the Old Testament into Aramaic is known as a targum. Such translation was necessitated after the Babylonian Captivity when Aramaic replaced Hebrew as the language of the Jews. These were first done only orally and were finally committed to writing several centuries after the time of Christ. A number of these targums exist and some are of greater value than others in reflecting the Hebrew text with accuracy. There are also some Syriac, Latin and Greek (other than the Septuagint) versions known to the textual critics.

All the evidence available to the Old Testament textual critic points to the conclusion that the text of the Hebrew Bible has been preserved with an amazing care and accuracy. Confident that the very words of the book were from God, meticulous care was taken by its custodians as they preserved it for future generations. H. H. Rowley has written: "We may rest assured that the consonantal text of the Hebrew Bible, though not infallible, has been preserved with an accuracy perhaps unparalleled in any other Near-Eastern literature."[4]

Concerning the New Testament

As with the autographs of the Old Testament books, there are no original copies of the letters of Paul or the Gospels available for our handling and reading today.

> It is true that we do not possess any of the original manuscripts. Perhaps this is just as well, since the history of Christianity has shown a tendency to worship ancient relics. But this does not mean that we are any less certain about the original text. This writer is not aware that we have the original text (called autographs) of any important ancient document. But if an original was widely circulated early, was copied, was quoted, and was translated into different languages, it can be reconstructed by a comparison of the different witnesses. Actually, if only one witness had been kept by itself, that one

source might have been stolen and replaced by a substitute, whereas many independent witnesses, even if they are secondary, cannot be fabricated.[5]

A wealth of manuscript evidence is available to the textual critic in his study of the New Testament documents. Bruce M. Metzger[6] is a recognized authority in this field and informs us that there are approximately 5,000 Greek manuscripts available to the textual critic which contain all or part of the New Testament.

> Perhaps we can appreciate how wealthy the New Testament is in manuscript attestation if we compare the textual material for other ancient historical works. For Casear's *Gallic War* (composed between 58 and 50 BC) there are several extant MSS, but only nine or ten are good, and the oldest is some 900 years later than Caesar's day. Of the 142 books of the Roman History of Livy (59 BC-AD 17) only thirty-five survive; these are known to us from not more than twenty MSS of any consequence, only one of which, and that containing fragments of Books iii-vi, is as old as the fourth century . . . The History of Thucydides (*c.* 460-400 BC) is known to us from eight MSS, the earliest belonging to *c.* AD 900, and a few papyrus scraps, belonging to about the beginning of the Christian era. The same is true of the History of Herodotus (*c.* 480-425 BC). Yet no classical scholar would listen to an argument that the authenticity of Herodotus is in doubt because the earliest MSS of their works which are of any use to us are over 1,300 years later than the originals.[7]

The oldest and most important manuscripts of the New Testament known to us are written entirely in capital letters and are called *uncials*. There are approximately 300 of these available to textual critics. The oldest and best of all the uncials are the Vatican Manuscript (kept in the Vatican Library at Rome), the Sinaitic Manuscript (found in a monastery on Mt. Sinai) and the Alexandrian Manuscript (first known to modern scholars from Alexandria, Egypt). These three are all written on vellum and date from A.D. 300-450.

The next oldest manuscripts are those written in a smaller, running hand. Named for the style of writing employed in producing them, they are known as *cursives*. These all date from the ninth to the fifteenth centuries and number in excess of 2,500.

The very oldest materials of the New Testament text available to scholars are in the form of papyrus fragments. Because papyrus deteriorates in other climates, such fragments have been found only in Egypt. Although in some ways inferior to the uncial manuscripts mentioned earlier (due to the fact that they are not as complete), there is a sense in which they are superior to the uncials (in that they bear witness to the existence of New Testament materials at a very early date). For example, certain liberal scholars had argued that the Gospel of John was not written until the middle of the second century. But the John Rylands Fragment (P^{52}), containing a few verses from John's Gospel (John 19:31-33, 37, 38), is confidently dated within the first half of the second century and shows conclusively that a copy of the book was being circulated in Egypt within only a few years after it was written. This papyrus fragment is the oldest known piece of New Testament manuscript.

The Chester Beatty Papyri were found and published in the 1930s. These are the remains of three ancient collections of New Testament documents. The first group contains materials from the four Gospels and Acts and is designated P^{45}. The second group (P^{46}) is a large collection of the epistles of Paul. The third group (P^{47}) contains the text of Revelation 9-17. The Beatty Papyri date from the third century.

Within the last twenty years, the Bodmer Library of Geneva published an entire copy of the Gospel of John (P^{66}) which dates from about A.D. 200. The importance of this document is readily apparent. The same source has also published the earliest known copies of Jude and the epistles of Peter (P^{72}) dating from the third century. The entire text of the Gospels of Luke and John, dating from between A.D. 175 and 225, have also been published by the Bodmer Library (P^{75}).

All the evidence available to Biblical scholars confirms the reliability of the text available to students of the Word of God. Sir Frederic Kenyon, Director of the British Museum for twenty-one years and an eminent scholar in this field, has said:

> The interval then between the dates of original composition and the earliest extant evidence becomes so small as to be in fact negligible, as the last foundation for any doubt that the Scriptures have come down to us substantially as they were written has now been removed. Both the authenticity and the general integrity of the books of the New Testament may be regarded as finally established.[8]

Aside from the manuscripts already mentioned, there are three other important sources of information which add to our assurance that the New Testament books have been faithfully transmitted through the ages. First, there are the versions. Quite early in its history, the New Testament began to be translated into various languages for the sake of missionary work. Since these translations were made so early from Greek manuscripts very near the autographs in point of time, they are helpful to the textual critic in dealing with certain matters of importance. The three groups of translations which are of greatest significance are the Syriac versions, the Coptic (or Egyptian) versions and the Latin versions.

> There are problems in reconstructing the text from translations. Admittedly many idioms cannot be translated. But for checking the absence or presence of a given reading in the text being used by the translators, these versions are especially helpful. There is no portion of the Greek New Testament which cannot be checked "from the mouth of two or three witnesses" by these three translations.[9]

Second, there is the valuable body of writings from the "Church Fathers." These men wrote from the period at the end of the first century and shortly afterward. Although they were certainly not inspired men, they possessed copies of the inspired Scripture which, of course, were older than the manuscripts which remain to us. Since their writings treated topics of interest and controversy among the earliest believers, they naturally quoted many Scripture texts in the course of their discussions.

Some scholars assert that the entire text of the New Testament could be recovered from the multitude of Scripture quotations contained in the writings of these men.

Third, there is the evidence provided by the lectionaries. "The term *lection* refers to a selected passage of Scripture designed to be read in the public worship services, and thus a lectionary is a manuscript especially arranged in sections for this purpsoe."[10] As one would expect, most lectionaries are composed from the Gospels. A good many, however, contain readings from Acts and the New Testament epistles. Even though they do not date before the sixth century, the texts from which they quote were certainly older and they were evidently copied very carefully since they were intended for use in public worship. More than 1,800 lectionaries are known to scholars of the Biblical text and are of great worth.

Thus we can confidently say that we have more than adequate evidence to establish the fact that we have a trustworthy text of both the Old and New Testaments. The sixty-six books contained therein constitute the complete body of inspired literature known to men today and are "profitable for teaching, for reproof, for correction, for instruction which is in righteousness: that the man of God may be complete, furnished completely unto every good work."[11]

THE WORK OF TRANSLATION

Finally a word needs to be said in this chapter about the work of translation. Granted that we have dependable manuscripts of the Hebrew Old Testament and Greek New Testament, not many people are able to read these languages. Most of us have to depend on translations from the Hebrew and Greek manuscripts into our own native tongue. Might not something have been lost in the process? How can we be sure that we really have the Word of God in English?

To be sure, Bible translating is a human and uninspired endeavor. There is no such thing as an "inspired translation"; the terms "inspired" and "infallible" belong only to the autographs of the Biblical documents. As Clyde

Woods has written: "Because translating is a human endeavor, there is no Biblical translation so good that it cannot be criticized. On the other hand, there is probably no translation so poor but what one can learn from it what to do to be saved and to live a Christian life."[12]

The most trustworthy of the translations are the *standard translations*. These have special merit due to the fact that they have been produced by large translation committees composed of scholars from various backgrounds and religious affiliations. Such men did their work within the guidelines of accepted translation procedures and checked each other's work. This system minimizes the possibility of a man reading something into the text that is not actually there; it reduces the likelihood of having the translation "slanted" toward the theological view of the translator; it encourages a faithful translation of the actual Hebrew or Greek text without misrepresentation. The most widely known and used of the standard English translations are the King James Version, the American Standard Version and the Revised Standard Version. Each of these has its strengths and weaknesses and none is wholly beyond the possibility of improvement. Yet each is a highly accurate translation and one reading from any of them can be assured that he is actually reading the Word of God in English.

The past few years have witnessed the publication and distribution of a number of translations (or, more correctly, paraphrases) of the Word of God which are of limited or doubtful usefulness. Usually called "modern speech" translations, these have been produced not by scholarly committees but by individuals who have been able to freely read their theological presuppositions into their "translations." *The New Testament in Modern English* by J. B. Phillips, *Good News for Modern Man* by Robert Bratcher and *The Living Bible Paraphrased* by Kenneth Taylor are examples of such works and each has its glaring failures and total misrepresentations of the Biblical text along with certain good points which could be mentioned. If used at all, these should not be considered on the level of the standard translations and regarded as primary study texts;

they should be viewed as *commentaries* on the text rather than translations of it and used with extreme care.

Conclusion

We have God's Word in our possession. After revealing, confirming and recording the saving truth which constitutes the Bible, God has seen to its preservation and dissemination through the ages. Let us thank God for his great goodness and receive his Word with joy unto salvation!

CHAPTER XII

The Value of Sacred Scripture

The basic consideration in all religious matters is that of establishing the authority which will be the final standard in controversy. In order to settle any disputed matter, we must be able to appeal to an authority which all parties concerned will accept. For example, the federal government has established a Bureau of Standards in order to guarantee uniformity of weights and measures throughout this country. The scales and measuring devices of any person dealing with the public have to be periodically checked against the bureau's standards. Any variation must be corrected immediately. Similarly, if men would be accurate in their religious beliefs and teachings, they must have a standard of authority with which to compare them. This standard must be unquestionably true and reliable and any variation from it must be corrected immediately.

The Bible alone is sufficient to serve as such a standard for faith and practice. In this time of darkness and spiritual uncertainty, let every man say, "(God's) word is a lamp unto my feet, and light unto my path!" (Psa. 119:105).

THE NARROW CHOICE

The Bible's claim to inspiration pervades every part of the book. The Bible clearly claims that Moses, the author of the first five books of the Old Testament, spoke and wrote words given him directly by God. "And Jehovah said unto (Moses), Who hath made man's mouth? or who maketh a man dumb, or deaf, or seeing, or blind? is it not I, Jehovah? Now therefore go, and I will be with thy mouth, and teach thee what thou shalt speak." (Ex. 4:11-12). David likewise claimed to be speaking words given him by God when he said, "The Spirit of Jehovah spake by me, and his word was upon my tongue." (2 Sam. 23:2). And Jeremiah said, "Then Jehovah put forth his hand, and touched my mouth; and Jehovah said unto me, Behold, I have put my words in thy mouth." (Jer. 1:9). Furthermore, Jesus and the apostles claimed inspiration for the Old Testament in such passages as John 10:35 and 2 Peter 1:21.

The New Testament's claim to divine inspiration are equally as clear as those of the Old Testament. Jesus promised the apostles: "Howbeit when he, the Spirit of truth, is come, he shall guide you into all the turth: for he shall not speak from himself; but what things soever he shall hear, these shall he speak . . ." (John 16:13-14). Jesus thus authenticated the New Testament books even before the apostles and other Spirit-filled men wrote them. He promised that these men would be guided into the truth, the whole truth and nothing but the truth! Christians are therefore correct in regarding the New Testament as a verbally inspired and inerrant revelation of the will of God to man!

Paul laid clear claim to speaking forth the Word of God as opposed to human wisdom or personal opinions. "And for this cause we also thank God without ceasing, that, when ye received from us the word of the message, even the word of God, ye accepted it not as the word of men, but, as it is in truth, the word of God, which also worketh in them that believe." (1 Thess. 2:13).

The Bible's claims for itself are too clear to be misunderstood. This book claims to be an inerrant, divine revelation. It claims to be the very Word of God. We are limited to a very narrow choice insofar as our attitude toward the Bible is concerned. Either the Bible is a worthless fraud and Jesus Christ is an imposter or else the Bible is the written and inerrant Word of God. Fulfilled prophecies in the Bible, its view of God and man, its relation to science and history, its unity and its unique ability to meet man's needs combine to lead the thinking person to the irresistable conclusion that *the Bible is exactly what it claims to be.*

Since it is true that the Bible is from God and is therefore authoritative over all men, the following propositions are necessarily true: the Bible is an unshakable foundation for our faith, it is our only hope for religious unity and it demands our unwavering obedience. Let us examine each of these points in its turn.

Sure Foundation for Our Faith

First, the Bible is an unshakable foundation for our faith. Man wants something more than philosophical hypotheses, theological speculation and educated guesses with regard to spiritual considerations that pertain to his eternal life and fellowship with God throughout unending ages. Each of us wants to be confident enough to say, "I am not ashamed; for I know him whom I have believed, and I am persuaded that he is able to guard that which I have committed unto him against that day." (2 Tim. 1:12).

Thank God for the certainty which we have through the Bible! We can *know* the truth and *know* that we know it! We can know that there is a personal, all-powerful God. We can know that Jesus Christ is God's only begotten Son and our Savior. We can know that we have received divine salvation through Christ. How can we know all these things? The Word of God tells us so! There is a "Thus saith the Lord" for every tenet of our faith.

The apostles never wavered regarding Christ and his gospel. They proclaimed the same Jesus Christ to all men and announced the terms on which men could receive salvation from him. They spoke with power and assurance. For this reason, John could write, "If anyone cometh unto you, and bringeth not this teaching, receive him not into your house, and give him no greeting." (2 John 10). What a difference in this attitude of absolute assurance and the ever-vascillating attitude of the modernist who does not accept the Bible's claims about itself!

The Word of God, as did Jesus during his personal ministry, teaches with authority. There is no hesitancy, doubting or uncertain sound in the pages of the Bible. The Bible speaks with absolute finality on every one of man's spritual questions. It is the impregnable rock upon which we securely rest our faith.

Basis for Religious Unity

Second, the Bible is our only hope for religious unity. The confusion and division of religious people in our day is the result of using different standards of authority. Some are guided by the traditions of the past. If a given doctrine has been around for a long time, its mere age seems to give it a flavor of respectability. Or if the members of a certain family have been members of such-and-such church for several generations, their beliefs and practices are seldom seriously questioned by the present generation. Others depend on the authority of learned men. If a man is respected as an authority in a particular field which he has studied, people are prone to believe that his opinions about any matter are authoritative. Thus some are heard to say, "But so-and-so said this and I believe he knows what he is talking about" or "Our preacher said this is right and he ought to know." Still others take as their authority such things as dreams, feelings or imaginations. This sort of person is the one who says, "Well, I am satisfied with my belief and am not interested in what you have to say."

The true guide in religion is the Word of God! The prophet Jeremiah said, "O Jehovah, I know that the way of man is not in himself; it is not in man that walketh to direct his steps." (Jer. 10:23). He recognized, as all must eventually, that man is not able to guide himself in religion. We must be able to appeal to a higher authority.

Solomon, in Proverbs 14:12, has pointed out the danger of man's effort to establish his own authority in religion: "There is a way which seemeth right unto a man; but the end thereof are the ways of death." Yes, it is extremely dangerous for any man to try to guide himself. Not only does the Bible declare this fact, but human experience teaches the same thing. There are over three hundred different denominations in the United States. Each is different from the other; yet each claims to rest on the authority of God. The problem is this: Different people recognize different standards of authority. If we would be united as the people of God, we must all return to the God-ordained standard in religion—the Bible.

The Bible is a reliable guide. In fact, it is the only reliable guide and standard of authority for our age and every age. "The law of Jehovah is perfect, restoring the soul: the testimony of Jehovah is sure, making wise the simple." (Psa. 19:7).

Was Jesus born of a virgin? Must one be baptized in order to be saved? What is the work of the church? How may we answer these questions so as to have general agreement? What one man thinks about the matter is of no more value than what his opponent thinks about it. But, since it has been demonstrated that the Bible is God's Word, it therefore becomes our final authority in deciding all matters of doctrine and practice. Let us seek a definitive answer to our spiritual questions by asking, with Paul, "What saith the scripture?" (Rom. 4:3.) When God's word has spoken on a given matter, there is no need to seek additional testimony. Man simply needs to hear and heed the Scriptures.

The Bible is the final court of appeal. It must settle every religious problem and answer every spiritual question. This was certainly the significance of Christ's statement when he said, "He that rejecteth me, and receiveth not my sayings, hath one that judgeth him: the word that I spake, the same shall judge him in the last day." (John 12:48).

The plea for men to accept the Bible alone as their guide in religion is both reasonable and welcome to those who examine it thoughtfully. Only when men accept this view of the Bible and its authority can there be any realistic hope of unity.

The Bible's Claims Upon Us

Third, the Bible demands our attention, careful study and obedience. A book so totally unique as the Bible is bound to make unique demands upon those to whom it has been entrusted. This, indeed, is the case with the Word of God.

The Bible declares men to be lost in sin and doomed to eternal punishment. What must man do to be saved? The inspired and authoritative answer comes, "Repent ye, and be baptized every one of you in the name of Jesus Christ unto the remission of your sins." (Acts 2:38). Since the Bible is true and binding, there is no alternative to these requirements. Any who refuse to obey them will remain in their sins and condemnation. Those who do repent and are baptized *know* they are saved. How? The Word of God says so!

How shall the saved person live? How shall he use his talents in service to the Lord? What spiritual duties are bound on him? The Scriptures give authoritative answers to these questions. Galatians 5:19-21 specifies certain things which must constantly be avoided. On the other hand, there are certain "fruits of the Spirit" which must be perpetually produced in the Christian's life. (Gal. 5:22-23). Regular worship, prayer and further study of the Bible assist the child of God in his spiritual life. In all things the will of God must have priority over one's own will. (Cf. Matt. 6:33).

No man who has access to a copy of the Bible can plead ignorance of God's will! The Scriptures leave one without excuse! God has revealed his will and communicated his divinely-ordained requirements for salvation through the written Word. Woe unto the person who refuses to take the time and expend the necessary energy to learn and obey them. To turn one's back on the Bible is to turn away from the God who authored it.

We must approach the Bible with the attitude, "Speak, Jehovah; for thy servant heareth." (1 Sam. 3:9). We must study it with the prayer, "Teach me, O Jehovah, the way of thy statutes; and I shall keep it unto the end." (Psa. 119:33).

BIBLIOLATRY?

Those who accept the plea set forth in this volume for a recognition of the inspired and authoritative character of the Bible are frequently accused of being bibliolators, i.e., people who worship the Bible rather than the God which the Bible reveals. Is it possible to worship God without placing absolute trust in the words he has spoken? Can a man love God and be indifferent to his Word?

The Psalmist exclaimed, "Thy law do I love." (Psa. 119:113). Was he a bibliolator? Do I become such because I love the Bible? It is impossible to separate our worship of God from our love of his Word! The charge of bibliolatry is merely an effort on the part of modernists to divert attention from their obvious lack of respect for the Bible.

We do not worship the Bible. We worship God—according to the instructions he has given in his Word. I am sure that we need not fear over-reverence of God's holy truth, but insufficient reverence.

CONCLUSION

God's will was once revealed through chosen men like Paul, Peter and John. Now his will is contained in an inspired book, the Bible. We are under obligation to study that book that we might have faith, for "belief cometh of hearing and hearing by the word of Christ." (Rom. 10:17).

He who has ears to hear, let him hear the Word of God and be saved!

Footnotes

CHAPTER ONE

[1]Gordon D. Kaufman, "What Shall We Do With the Bible?" *Interpretation*, XXV (January, 1971), 96.

[2]Emil Brunner, *The Theology of Crisis* (New York: Charles Scribner's Sons, 1930), p. 41.

[3]C. H. Dodd, *The Authority of the Bible* (London: Nisbet and Co., Ltd., 1955), p. 233.

[4]Karl Barth, *Church Dogmatics*, I, 2, "The Doctrine of the Word of God," trans. G. T. Thomson and Harold Knight (New York: Charles Scribner's Sons, 1956), pp. 528-29.

[5]C. H. Dodd, *Epistle of Paul to the Romans* (New York: Harper and Row, n.d.), p. xxxv.

CHAPTER TWO

[1]Dewey M. Beegle, *The Inspiration of Scripture* (Philadelphia: Westminster Press, 1963), p. 187.

[2]William Sanday, *The Oracles of God* (London: Longmans, Green and Co., 1891), p. 47.

[3]John Murray, "The Attestation of Scripture," *The Infallible Word*, edited by N. B. Stonehouse and Paul Woolley (Grand Rapids: Wm. B. Eerdmans Pub. Co., 1946), p. 23.

CHAPTER THREE

[1]Any *one* of the internal evidences of inspiration to be discussed in this book could be adequately explicated so as to be sufficient evidence within itself to establish the thesis of this book. The enumeration of *many* evidences does not make the conclusion more true, but such a marshaling of evidence does make the case more obvious and impressive.

[2]Appreciation is expressed to Thomas B. Warren for providing the basic structure of the syllogism used in this chapter and adapted for use in subsequent chapters.

[3]Bernard Ramm, *Protestant Christian Evidences* (Chicago: Moody Press, 1965), p. 81.

[4]W. E. Vine, *Expository Dictionary of New Testament Words* (Westwood, N. J.: Fleming H. Revell Company, 1962), III, 221.

[5]E. P. M'Ilvaine, *The Evidences of Christianity*, p. 238; as quoted in Ramm, *op. cit.*, p. 82.
[6]John H. Gerstner, *Reasons for Faith* (New York: Harper and Row, 1960), p. 115.

CHAPTER FOUR

[1]C. J. Sharp, *Why We Believe* (Cincinnati: Standard Publishing Co., 1932), pp. 12-13.
[2]Hugo McCord, *From Heaven or From Men?* (Austin, Texas: Firm Foundation Publishing House, n.d.), p. 91.
[3]Floyd E. Hamilton, *The Basis of Christian Faith* (New York: Harper & Row, 1964), p. 159.
[4]Rene Pache, *The Inspiration and Authority of Scripture*, translated by Helen I. Needham (Chicago: Moody Press, 1969), p. 117.
[5]*Ibid.*, p. 119.

CHAPTER FIVE

[1]Robert Camp, "Mistakes the Bible Does Not Make," *The Spiritual Sword*, I (October, 1969), 12. (Note: The student would profit greatly from reading this entire article.)
[2]See comments and footnote references in R. K. Harrison, *Introduction to the Old Testament* (Grand Rapids: William B. Eerdmans Pub. Co., 1969), pp. 607-10.
[3]See the extended treatment of this subject by S. I. McMillen, M. D., *None of These Diseases* (Westwood, N. J.: Fleming H. Revell Co., 1963).
[4]Don England, *Evidences of Inspiration* (Searcy, Arkansas: Privately published, 1971), p. 29; Cf. P. Ghalioungui, *Magic and Medical Science in Ancient Egypt* (Loudon: Hodder and Stoughton, 1963).
[5]B. L. Gordon, M.D., *Medicine Throughout Antiquity*, quoted in England, *op. cit.*, p. 30.

CHAPTER SIX

[1]Paul E. Little, *Know Why You Believe* (Downers Grove, Illinois: Inter-Varsity Press, 1968), pp. 95-96.
[2]H. J. Muller, article in *Scientific American* (Nov., 1955), p. 59.
[3]Quotations from *Herald and News*, Klamath Falls, Oregon, Dec. 27, 1971.
[4]Little, *op. cit.*, pp. 94-95.
[5]McCord, *op. cit.*, pp. 80-81.

CHAPTER SEVEN

[1]John Murray, *op. cit.*, pp. 46-47.
[2]Joseph P. Free, *Archaeology and Bible History* (Wheaton, Ill.: Scripture Press Publications, Inc., 1969), pp. 1-2.
[3]William F. Albright, *The Archaeology of Palestine*, Rev. ed. (Hammondsworth, Middlesex: Pelican Books, 1960), pp. 127-28.
[4]Nelson Glueck, *Rivers in the Desert; History of Neteg* (Philadelphia: Jewish Publications Society of America, 1969), p. 31.
[5]Millar Burrows, *What Mean These Stones?* (New York: Meridian Books, 1956), p. 291.
[6]Julius Wellhausen, *Prolegomena to the History of Israel*, pp. 318-19, quoted in Charles F. Pfeiffer, *The Patriarchal Age* (Grand Rapids: Baker Book House, 1964), p. 12.
[7]Burrows, *op. cit.*, pp. 258-59.

[8]Free, *op. cit.*, pp. 107-9.

[9]Allen Bowman, *Is the Bible True?* (Westwood, N. J.: Fleming H. Revell Company, 1965), pp. 166-67.

[10]So popular a historical work as Will Durant, *The Story of Civilization: Part III, Caesar and Christ* (New York: Simon and Schuster, 1944), p. 588 contains a reference to this "discrepancy" in Luke's record of the birth of Christ.

[11]Because of an error made in computing the ancient calendar, Christ was not born in A.D. 1 (as we now compute dates) but was actually born a few years B.C. Quirinius' first governorship of Syria was around 6 B.C. The exact date of Christ's birth is, of course, not known to us.

[12]R. C. H. Lenski, *The Interpretation of St. Luke's Gospel* (Minneapolis: Augsburg Publishing House, 1946), p. 174.

[13]F. F. Bruce, "Archaeological Confirmation of the New Testament," in Carl F. H. Henry, ed., *Revelation and the Bible* (Grand Rapids: Baker Book House, 1958), p. 325.

[14]William Ramsay, *St. Paul the Traveler and Roman Citizens* (Grand Rapids: Baker Book House, 1962), pp. 7-8.

[15]Millar Burrows, *The Dead Sea Scrolls* (New York: Viking Press, 1955), p. 320.

CHAPTER EIGHT

[1]Clark H. Pinnock, "Our Source of Authority: The Bible," *Bibliotheca Sacra*, CXXIV (April-June, 1967), 151.

[2]Loraine Boettner, *Studies in Theology* (Philadelphia: Presbyterian and Reformed Publishing Co., 1947), p. 28.

[3]Clark H. Pinnock, *Biblical Revelation—The Foundation of Christian Theology* (Chicago: Moody Press, 1971), p. 178.

[4]The material concerning the six sources of alleged errors in the Bible appears, in only slightly different form, in Rubel Shelly, *Simple Studies in Christian Evidences* (Memphis: Simple Studies Publishing Company, 1970), pp. 62-65.

CHAPTER NINE

[1]Dewey M. Beegle, *Scripture, Tradition, and Infallibility* (Grand Rapids: William B. Eerdmans Publishing Company, 1973). This book is a rearranged and enlarged version of Dewey M. Beegle, *The Inspiration of Scripture* (Philadelphia: Westminster Press, 1963).

[2]Beegle, *The Inspiration of Scripture*, p. 187.

[3]Beegle, *Scripture, Tradition, and Infallibility*, p. 197. (All subsequent citations from Beegle are from this volume.)

[4]Bowman, *op. cit.*, pp. 125-26.

[5]Floyd E. Hamilton, *op. cit.*, p. 174.

[6]Edward J. Young, "Are the Scriptures Inerrant?" in *The Bible —The Living Word of Revelation*, ed. by Merrill C. Tenney (Grand Rapids: Zondervan Pub. House, 1968), p. 113.

[7]Beegle, *op. cit.*, p. 180.

[8]*Ibid.*, p. 181.

[9]Second Kings 15:19 establishes the fact that Menahem's reign was in progress when "Pul the King of Assyria" ("Pul" was the Babylonian nickname for Tiglath-pileser III) exacted tribute from Isarel. But if Pekah's dates are altered by counting back from 722 B.C., then Menahem could not have been reigning when this tribute was paid (ca. 743 B.C.).

[10]Cf. 2 Kings 15:32; 16:1.

[11] Beegle, *op. cit.*, p. 184.

[12] In setting forth a reasonable solution to the difficulty of the reign of Pekah, I am closely following H. J. Cook, "Pekah," *Vetus Testamentum*, XIV (April, 1964), 121-35. The same suggestion in much briefer form is found in H. B. MacLean, "Pekah," *The Interpreter's Dictionary of the Bible*, ed. by George Arthur Buttrick (New York: Abingdon Press, 1962), III, 708.

[13] The difference of one year which frequently appears in dates assigned to these periods of antiquity is due to the fact that Judah and Israel used different systems for reckoning the years of a king's reign. At the time of the division of the kingdom, Israel followed a nonaccession-year method of computation and continued in this manner until the end of the ninth century B.C. when the change to accession-year system was made. Judah, however, used the accession-year method until the middle of the ninth century B.C. and then changed over to the nonaccession-year system.

[14] *Ibid.*, pp. 127-28.

[15] Cf. Bernhard W. Anderson, *Understanding the Old Testament*, 2nd ed. (Englewood Cliffs, N. J.: Prentice-Hall, Inc., 1966), p. 198, and Norman K. Gottwald, *A Light to the Nations* (New York: Harper and Row, 1959), p. 247.

[16] Cook, *op. cit.* p. 132.

[17] W. L. Reed, "Ephraim," *The Interpreter's Dictionary of the Bible*, ed. by George Arthur Buttrick (New York: Abingdon Press, 1962), II, 120.

[18] Cook, *op. cit.*, pp. 134-35.

[19] Cf. H. R. Thiele, *The Mysterious Numbers of the Hebrew Kings* (Chicago: University of Chicago Press, 1951).

[20] *Ibid.*, p. xxiii.

[21] Beegle, *op. cit.*, p. 184.

[22] For a brief survey of some of the more recent suggestions on this problem and the offering of his own unique approach to it see Appendix I: "The Reign of Hezekiah" in Edward J. Young, *The Book of Isaiah*, Vol. II (Grand Rapids: Wm. B. Eerdmans Pub. Co., 1969), pp. 540f.

[23] K. A. Kitchen and T. C. Mitchell, "Chronology of the Old Testament," *The New Bible Dictionary*, ed. by J. D. Douglas (Grand Rapids: Wm. B. Eerdmans Pub. Co., 1962), pp. 212-23.

[24] Beegle, *The Inspiration of Scripture*, p. 51.

[25] *Ibid.*

[26] Beegle, *Scripture, Tradition, and Infallibility*, p. 186.

[27] *Ibid.*

[28] *Ibid.*

[29] *Ibid.*, p. 186-87.

[30] Gen. 1:1.

[31] Gen. 5:1.

[32] Matt. 1:8.

[33] Young, "Are the Scriptures Inerrant?", p. 113.

CHAPTER TEN

[1] The speech is recorded in rather full form in Acts 7:2-53.

[2] Beegle, *op. cit.*, p. 190.

[3] Edward J. Young, *Thy Word is Truth* (Grand Rapids: Wm. B. Eerdmans Pub. Co., 1957), pp. 176-77.

[4]Beegle, *op. cit.*, p. 188.
[5]*Ibid.*, p. 55.
[6]F. F. Bruce, *Commentary on the Book of the Acts* (Grand Rapids: Wm. B. Eerdmans Publishing Co., 1954), p. 146n.
[7]Support for this view is alleged to be contained in the statement of Joshua 24:2: "And Joshua said unto all the people, Thus saith Jehovah, the God of Israel, Your fathers dwelt of old time beyond the River, even Terah. The father of Abraham, and the father of Nahor: and they served other gods."
[8]The rendering of Acts 7:4 in the RSV as opposed to "when his father was dead" (in both the ASV and KJV).
[9]J. W. McGarvey, *New Commentary on Acts of Apostles* (1892 ed. Reprinted; Delight, Ark.: Gospel Light Pub. Co., n.d.), pp. 117-18n.
[10]Young, *Thy Word is Truth*, p. 178.
[11]McGarvey, *op. cit.*, p. 118n.
[12]Beegle, *op. cit.*, p. 189.
[13]Bruce, *op. cit.*, pp. 148-49.
[14]Beegle, *op. cit.*, p. 190.
[15]McGarvey, *op. cit.*, p. 121n.
[16]Beegle, *op. cit.*, p. 189.
[17]This would, of course, allow for the interesting possibility that Jacob also was removed from Hebron to Shechem. This would allow the common English rendering of the Greek text of Acts 7:16 to stand and eliminate the apparent contradiction between Acts and Genesis by means of two burials having been involved with the bodies of both Jacob and his eleven sons.
[18]Beegle, *op. cit.*, p. 190.
[19]*Ibid.*
[20]R. C. H. Lenski, *The Interpretation of the Acts of the Apostles* (Minneapolis: Augsburg Publishing House, 1934).
[21]Bruce, *Acts*, p. 149n.
[22]Beegle, *op. cit.*, p. 191.
[23]Cf. Acts 7:6 where Stephen states that Israel was in Egyptian bondage for 400 years. Here Stephen evidently used a round number to refer to the period which actually totaled 430 years.
[24]Beegle, *op. cit.*, p. 192.
[25]W. Arndt, *Bible Difficulties* (1932 ed. Reprint; St. Louis: Concordia Publishing House, 1971), pp. 79-80.
[26]Young, *Thy Word is Truth*, pp. 181-82.
[27]*Ibid.*, p. 182.
[28]Beegle, *op. cit.*, p. 191.
[29]Beegle, *op. cit.*, p. 192.
[30]Cf. Gen. 28:13; 32:9; 48:16; 50:24; Ex. 6:3; 32:13; Deut. 1:8; 9:5, 27; 29:13; 30:20; 1 Chron. 29:18; Matt. 22:32; Mark 12:26; Acts 3:13.
[31]Beegle, loc. cit.
[32]*Ibid.*, p. 193.
[33]Robert Preus, "Notes on the Inerrancy of Scripture," *Bulletin of the Evangelical Theological Society*, VIII (Autumn, 1965), 132.
[34]Norval Geldenhuys, *Commentary on the Gospel of Luke* (Grand Rapids: Wm. B. Eerdmans Publishing Company, 1951), p. 568n.
[35]Beegle, *op. cit.*, pp. 193-94.

[30]*Ibid.*, p. 194.
[31]*Ibid.*, p. 177.
[32]*Ibid.*, p. 179.
[33]R. C. H. Lenski, *The Interpretation of the Epistles of St. Peter, St. John and St. Jude* (Columbus, Ohio: Wartburg Press, 1945), p. 640.
[34]William G. Moorehead, "Jude, The Epistle of," *International Standard Bible Encyclopedia*, ed. by James Orr (Grand Rapids: Wm. B. Eerdmans Pub. Co., 1939), III, 1771.
[35]Cf. Gen. 5:4-18 for the tracing of genealogies which places Enoch in the seventh generation from Adam.
[36]Only a few fragments of this work remain and the story in question here is not related in any of them. References to this account in the *Assumption of Moses* are contained in the writings of certain "Church Fathers" who apparently had access to the document.
[37]Beegle, *op. cit.*, p. 180.
[38]B. B. Warfield, *The Inspiration and Authority of the Bible* (Philadelphia: Presbyterian and Reformed Pub. Co., 1948), p. 440.

CHAPTER ELEVEN

[1]R. K. Harrison, *op. cit.*, p. 212.
[2]R. Laird Harris, "How Reliable is the Old Testament Text?" in *Can I Trust My Bible?* (Chicago: Moody Press, 1936), p. 124.
[3]Gleason L. Archer, Jr., *A Survey of Old Testament Introduction* (Chicago: Moody Press, 1964), p. 19.
[4]H. H. Rowley, *The Old Testament in Modern Study* (Oxford: Clarendon Press, 1961), p. 25.
[5]J. W. Roberts, "The Authenticity of the Scriptures," in *Pillars of Faith*, ed. by Herman O. Wilson and Morris M. Womack (Grand Rapids: Baker Book House, 1973), p. 144.
[6]Bruce M. Metzger, *The Text of the New Testament* (Oxford: Oxford University Press, 1968).
[7]F. F. Bruce, *The New Testament Documents: Are They Reliable?* Fifth Revised Edition (Grand Rapids: William B. Eerdmans Publishing Company, 1971), pp. 16-17.
[8]Frederic G. Kenyon, *The Bible and Archaeology* (New York: Harper and Bros., 1940), p. 288.
[9]Roberts, *op. cit.*, p. 147.
[10]Neil R. Lightfoot, *How We Got the Bible* (Grand Rapids: Baker Book House, 1972), p. 39. The student interested in a readable and reliable source of more information on the transmission and translation of the Bible should read this book in its entirety.
[11]People sometimes ask why it is that the Catholic Bible contains more books than the sixty-six which are generally recognized as canonical. These Apocryphal books do not even claim to be the Word of God, are obviously inferior in content and value to the canonical books, were never accepted as God-given literature by the Jews or early Christians. No one need fear that our Bibles with sixty-six books are lacking or incomplete!
[12]Clyde M. Woods, "The Circulation, Translation and Survival of the Bible," *The Spiritual Sword*, I (January, 1970), 18.